Your Primary
School-based
Experience

A Guide to Outstanding Placements

SECOND EDITION

**CRITICAL
TEACHING**

You might also like the following books in our Critical Teaching series:

Beyond Early Reading
David Waugh and Sally Neaum
978-1-909330-41-2 September 2013

Beyond Early Writing
David Waugh, Adam Bushnell and Sally Neaum (eds)
978-1-909682-93-1 June 2015

Digital Literacy for Primary Teachers
Moira Savage and Anthony Barnett
978-1-909682-61-0 February 2015

Enriching Primary English
Jonathan Glazzard and Jean Palmer
978-1-909682-49-8 January 2015

Inclusive Primary Teaching (2nd edn)
Janet Goepel, Helen Childerhouse and Sheila Sharpe
978-1-910391-38-9 September 2015

Practical Ideas for TeachingPrimary Science
Vivian Cooke and Colin Howard
978-1-909682-29-0 June 2014

Reflective Primary Teaching
Tony Ewens
978-1-909682-17-7 May 2014

Teaching and Learning Early Years Mathematics: Subject and Pedagogic Knowledge
Mary Briggs
978-1-909330-37-5 September 2013

Teaching Systematic Synthetic Phonics and Early English
Jonathan Glazzard and Jane Stokoe
978-1-909330-09-2 March 2013

Understanding and Enriching Problem Solving in Primary Mathematics
Patrick Barmby and David Bolden
978-1-909330-69-6 May 2014

Most of our titles are also available in a range of electronic formats. To order please go to our website www.criticalpublishing.com or contact our distributor, NBN International, 10 Thornbury Road, Plymouth PL6 7PP, telephone 01752 202301 or email orders@nbninternational.com.

Your Primary
School-based
Experience

A Guide to Outstanding Placements

SECOND EDITION

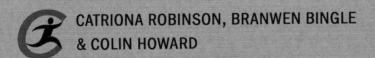

CATRIONA ROBINSON, BRANWEN BINGLE
& COLIN HOWARD

**CRITICAL
TEACHING**

First published in 2013 by Critical Publishing Ltd

Second edition published in 2015

British Library Cataloguing in Publication Data
A CIP record for this book is available from the British Library

ISBN: 978-1-910391-13-6

This book is also available in the following e-book formats:

MOBI ISBN: 978-1-910391-14-3
EPUB ISBN: 978-1-910391-15-0
Adobe e-book ISBN: 978-1-910391-16-7

Cover design by Out of House
Text design by Greensplash Limited
Project Management by Out of House Publishing
Printed and bound in Great Britain by 4edge Limited, Essex

Critical Publishing
152 Chester Road
Northwich
CW8 4AL
www.criticalpublishing.com

Contents

Acknowledgements

Material from the Department for Education is Crown Copyright and is gratefully reproduced free of charge under the terms of the Open Government Licence.

We are grateful to Professor Chris Robertson, for encouraging us to write for Critical Publishing. We have benefited from the informal conversations held with colleagues, in particular the support given by Rachel Barrell when writing about teaching inclusively.

We are indebted to the many students and tutors whose stories have been told throughout the book and likewise to Julia Morris from Critical Publishing for her editorial skills. The constructive critical feedback has been supportive and Julia has made the process of writing and redrafting chapters seamless and efficient. Without her patience, along with polite prompting, the task to complete the book would still be in hand.

Finally this book would not have been possible without the support of our immediate families. Above all, thank you to our respective spouses, Stewart, Keiran and Angela for their unwavering support, reassurance and patience. They each deserve a medal!

Meet the authors

Catriona Robinson is a principal lecturer and an Associate Head of the Institute of Education at the University of Worcester. As a tutor she has supported undergraduate and PGCE trainees and has worked with them in placement settings. In addition she has developed training programmes for school mentors, and been the Primary Partnership Manager and Acting Head of Primary Strategic Partnerships, investigating new and more creative placements for trainees. She has previously lead the Graduate Teacher Programme and the Assessment Only Route. Her research interests include teachers' professional identity, and the student voice in higher education and she is currently undertaking her professional doctorate.

Branwen Bingle is a senior lecturer in primary ITE at the University of Worcester. Always a committed mentor of students in the classroom, Branwen moved from primary teaching into ITE in 2008. She has been a supply teacher and support assistant for Service Children's Education; a basic skills tutor working with adults in the military; a private day nursery teacher working with three and four year olds; a secondary English teacher working across Key Stages 3 and 4, including the teaching of GCSE; and a subject leader for literacy in two middle schools. She is currently researching various aspects of teachers' professional identity.

Colin Howard is a senior lecturer in primary ITE at the University of Worcester. He has been involved in primary education for over 24 years, of which 14 years were as a successful head teacher in both small village and large primary school settings. He has been involved in inspecting schools for the Diocese of Hereford as a S48 SIAS inspector. His PhD is linked to his interest in the influence that school buildings have upon their stakeholders.

Introduction

If you are reading this, you have probably been accepted onto a teacher training course – in which case, congratulations! You are about to embark on an exciting and rewarding journey and enter a vibrant and ever-changing profession. You will doubtlessly be anticipating the school-based element of your course, although you may have some reservations about entering the province of a primary school in the role of a trainee teacher. This book serves to reassure you at each stage of your school experience, whether it is prior to starting a school placement or while fully immersed in teaching in your current placement setting. It endeavours to answer some of your more pressing questions in the 'Frequently asked questions' section and explains current terminology in a concise glossary.

The book is suitable for you if you are about to start your school-based experience / placement and useful no matter what route you are taking into the profession. For example it is appropriate for those on a three- or four-year undergraduate programme, a traditional one-year PGCE or a School Direct Training programme. Likewise for those on employment-based routes, you will glean useful information from the book to help you with your transition, perhaps as a higher level teaching assistant (HLTA) who is undertaking a trainee teacher placement in a second school. Equally if you are on the Teach First programme, once your intensive training has been completed you will be looking forward to your employment in school and this book will assist you in your preparation.

This second edition has been fully updated throughout and in particular includes references to the latest version of the national curriculum, extended thinking tasks in each main chapter and new suggestions for further reading.

Chapter 1 centres on being a reflective practitioner and talks about the reflective cycle and how this helps to produce a good teacher; one who continually develops and improves. Different theoretical perspectives of reflection are considered, eg Kolb. Discussion surrounds the complexities of teaching and learning and reveals how reflection will help you reshape your past, current and future teaching experiences in order to improve your practice.

In Chapter 2, the focus is on your personal professional attributes and what it means to be professional. It explores your values, interpersonal skills, emotional intelligence, attitude, expectations and ways in which to address conflict and to communicate. It considers professionalism and professional identity along with your personal conduct in and out of school. Self-evaluation informs the debate surrounding your professionalism and the attributes required for you to make an outstanding teacher.

Chapter 3 discusses the practicalities of placement, for example the dress code, when to arrive, staff room etiquette and involvement with extra-curricular activities. It considers the relationship between you and your mentor; this is examined in greater depth in Chapter 4. In addition consideration is given to paired placements, as the chapter evaluates the positives that might arise from working closely with another trainee.

A focus on collaborative professional partnerships is developed in Chapter 4. This involves working with other adults including teaching and non-teaching staff, mentors, parents, carers and outside agencies. In particular a significant amount of this chapter reflects on the importance of the trainee/mentor relationship and the need for you to get it right from the outset. The chapter sets out differing perspectives of the professional mentoring relationship to emphasise its significance.

At the heart of the book are several chapters (Chapters 5, 7 and 8) that address the key national priorities for the primary phase. Chapter 5 considers how to manage classroom behaviour particularly through a child-centred approach to discipline. It concentrates on school behaviour policies and the consistent implementation of rewards and sanctions that you might be expected to employ in a placement setting.

Chapter 6 critically evaluates planning, differentiation and assessment. References are made to the new Early Years Foundation Stage (EYFS) curriculum and current assessment strategies across all age phases which clearly link with Chapter 1 on reflection. Most importantly it discusses assessment and its prominence in informing planning and driving forward learning and teaching within the classroom.

Chapter 7 specifically addresses the teaching of the core subjects, English, mathematics and science, and provides some useful checklists for planning, teaching and assessment in these areas. It considers resources, different teaching styles and teaching across the different key stages. The current curriculum for KS1 and 2 is central to the teaching of the core subjects; and this is set in the context of the new national curriculum (DfE, 2014).

Inclusive teaching is scrutinised in Chapter 8, which explores the special educational needs (SEN) arena and English as an additional language (EAL), including a range of social, cultural and religious backgrounds. Chapters 5, 7 and 8 are significant because they relate to the Ofsted inspection framework (2012) and the Teachers' Standards (2011), both of which are referred to within each chapter.

In the creative placements chapter (Chapter 9) innovative ways of using placements to enable trainees to develop as subject specialists are explored. For example your placement may be in an educational setting other than a school. It challenges you to think about the differences and similarities of working in alternative settings and the necessity of remaining professional no matter what setting you are placed within in order to address the new teaching standards.

Chapter 10 draws together previous chapters and illustrates what a good and outstanding trainee might look like, suggesting ways in which you can move from good to outstanding. It encourages you to think about 'taking risks' through a more creative and engaging way of teaching where the children's curiosity and enquiry leads to intensive extended learning. Case studies make clear what is required to achieve outstanding and encourage self-reflection so that you are equipped to make the next steps to becoming an outstanding teacher.

To conclude, Chapter 11 encourages you to critically reflect on your last placement in order to complete job applications and secure your first appointment as a newly qualified teacher (NQT). The chapter poses questions related to your subject strengths and how you might write your personal statement to address job and personal specifications. Finally it helps you to reflect on how to prepare for your NQT year and what level of support you should get through your induction year.

The closing sections of the book include frequently asked questions, a glossary of useful terms and acronyms, references and the index.

Chapters include links to the current Teachers' Standards, case studies, critical questions, chapter reflections, extended reflections, critical points and further reading. These learning features are provided to ensure you understand the text, to help you apply it to your own personal circumstances and to promote deeper thinking about the issues explored.

1 Reflection throughout practice

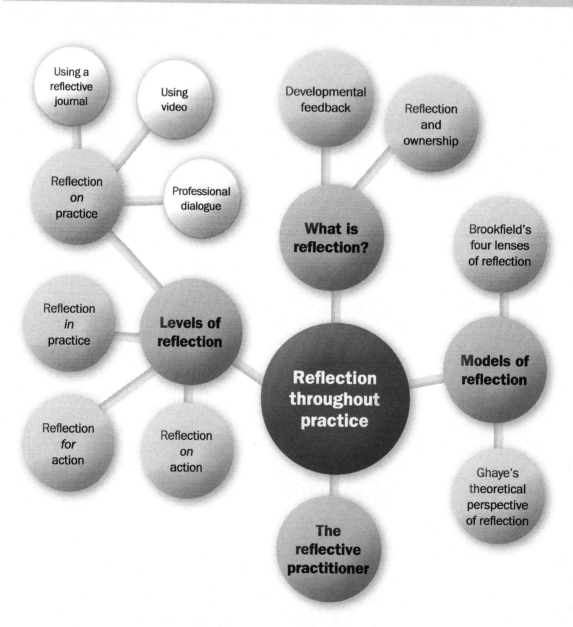

Using a reflective journal

Using video

Reflection *on* practice

Professional dialogue

Reflection *in* practice

Levels of reflection

Reflection *for* action

Reflection *on* action

Developmental feedback

Reflection and ownership

What is reflection?

Brookfield's four lenses of reflection

Reflection throughout practice

Models of reflection

Ghaye's theoretical perspective of reflection

The reflective practitioner

Teachers' Standards (DfE, 2011c)

2 Promote good progress and outcomes by pupils

- demonstrate knowledge and understanding of how pupils learn and how this impacts on teaching.

4 Plan and teach well-structured lessons

- reflect systematically on the effectiveness of lessons and approaches to teaching.

8 Fulfil wider professional responsibilities

- take responsibility for improving teaching through appropriate professional development, responding to advice and feedback from colleagues.

Introduction

Underpinning the effectiveness of this book is your ability to reflect on the critical questions and case studies raised throughout subsequent chapters. Therefore Chapter 1 seeks to enhance your reflection on practice related to a school context and to the contents of this book.

Fundamental to every successful teaching placement and indeed central to being a good or better teacher is the ability to reflect. This chapter introduces you to a number of theoretical models of reflection. These will assist you in becoming a proficient reflective practitioner who continually strives to develop and improve your practice in the classroom. You will be given the opportunity to critically reflect on the complexities of learning and teaching in order to reshape your past, present and future teaching experiences.

What is reflection?

There is much written about what constitutes reflection, when it occurs and the art of being a reflective practitioner. Fundamentally reflection is the skill of looking back at your and other teaching professionals' practice in order to identify elements that work well, to reveal avenues for action in order to effect a positive change. Ghaye and Ghaye (1998) regard reflection on action as a continuous and cyclical process. Ghaye later defines reflection as being a ... *skilful practice* (Ghaye, 2011, page 20) that draws upon experience in order to action and positively transform a situation. In the past, reflection has often focused on a deficit model whereby, either in isolation or with others, the negative aspects of practice are highlighted. All too often the focus is on targeting the areas for development that are having a negative effect on practice (developmental feedback). The issues are defined and consequently targets are set so as to repair what is broken. You might think that this is a level-headed starting point but building on strengths of your practice is equally important.

Consider the case studies below of two trainee teachers recounting their feedback following a lesson observation.

CASE STUDIES

Lisa's feedback

Well, the tutor sat me down after the lesson and asked me how I thought the lesson had gone. I thought it had gone pretty well. I mentioned that I had got through all the teaching that I had planned for the lesson which I was pleased with. The tutor then gave me my feedback. It was dreadful. There were so many issues with the lesson I didn't know where to begin to put things right. The tutor said I had no presence in the class and that my voice was weak. In addition he said that my pronunciation was not good. My pace was slow and I lacked enthusiasm. I am not sure that he said anything about what had gone well in the lesson and if he did, I wasn't listening. All the feedback that fell on my ears criticised my practice. It felt like a personal attack. I was mortified.

Sam's feedback

After my science lesson, the mentor asked what aspects of my practice I was happy with in the lesson. I was unsure as to the exact parts of the lesson that had gone well but thought the children had all been engaged. The mentor then asked me to pinpoint what had enabled the children to remain focused and on task in the lesson but I found it difficult to pinpoint the factors that had contributed. The mentor then itemised all the aspects of my practice that had facilitated the children's engagement. The mentor said that I had kept the teaching lively and not too much time was spent on teacher talk. The children had short activities to complete in the first part of the lesson and afterwards they led their own investigation which the mentor said gave them ownership. I was really pleased with the feedback but I was unsure as to what I needed to do next time to make my practice better.

Critical questions

» *Which feedback would you react best to?*

» *Which feedback would help you to develop your practice?*

» *Do you react better to developmental feedback or feedback that celebrates the positives?*

» *Think back to some feedback you have already received. (If you haven't started a placement yet, recall feedback on an essay or perhaps just from a friend.) What style of feedback was it? How did you react and how might you have reacted differently? Did you make any changes as a result of the feedback?*

Developmental feedback

Many trainee teachers take developmental feedback personally. In many ways this is a natural response, especially in the example of the first case study above where Lisa's voice and presence are called into question. When feedback is related to your character and personality, it is hard to de-personalise and view the feedback objectively. However, you need to disentangle yourself from the feedback and focus on how these points can be addressed in order to improve your practice. We all like to hear if our practice is good as this often motivates individuals. In the second case study Sam receives amplification of what is working well; however, he appears unable to appreciate that the positive feedback should empower him to build upon the best aspects of his practice (see Cooperrider and Whitney, 2005, in Taking it further). In contrast, he focuses his attention on the fact that he has not been told what elements of his practice are in need of development. In the initial stages of your teacher training, identifying rudiments of your practice which work well and areas for future development may well be difficult. Being a novice in the profession, you are probably conscious that you don't know what you don't know and therefore initially you will probably need explicit developmental feedback in order to move your practice forward (Loughran, 2000). This is perfectly acceptable and to be expected.

Critical questions

» How will you develop and change your practice if you receive feedback that solely celebrates what is working well?

» How will you respond and react if you hear feedback about your practice that you would rather not hear?

» What strategies might you need to put in place to help you address your feelings when receiving feedback?

Reflection and ownership

Nonetheless you ideally need to take ownership of the reflection upon your practice rather than relying on the feedback and reflection of others. This often comes with more experience; however, the sooner you become more effective and proficient in reflecting on your practice, potentially your progress will be realised more rapidly. Taking ownership of your reflection harnesses a powerful vehicle for change in your practice and is addressed later on in this chapter.

Trainee teachers often resort to highlighting features of their practice that are in need of development when asked to reflect upon the positive aspects of their practice. Consider the following case study.

CASE STUDY

Toni's reflection

A supervisory tutor asks a trainee teacher to tell them what aspects of the lesson went well. The trainee begins:

I was pleased that I had got extension activities prepared for the children today as I needed them. But that was because I had not planned enough for the lesson and the work was too easy for the children. I had not pitched the level of the work appropriately which meant the children finished too quickly and were not challenged. I should have checked with the class teacher when I was planning to see what the children already knew.

The tutor intervenes:

So what else worked well in today's lesson?

Critical questions

»   *What aspects of Toni's practice are going well?*

»   *What aspects of Toni's practice are in need of development?*

»   *How reflective is the trainee?*

»   *What targets would you set the trainee?*

»   *Why was it important for the tutor to intervene?*

As you can see from the recount above, Toni rapidly moves from reflecting upon the best elements of her practice to concentrating on the facets that require improvement. Through professional dialogue you should be made to probe your practice further in order to identify other characteristics of your practice that are effective. You could then in turn employ these more readily in practice so as to effect change.

This introduction has provided a brief summary of reflection, particularly in light of dialogue with and feedback from other professional colleagues. Now consider what you understand from the following questions.

Critical questions

»   *What is critical reflection?*

»   *What elements of critical reflection do you believe you will excel at?*

»   *Which aspects of critical reflection will need effort on your part?*

Models of reflection

This section illustrates some models that you might like to employ in order to assist in your reflection. Research around reflective models is widely available, although it is not possible to evaluate them all in this book. Therefore three key models have been included for your consideration. You will examine Brookfield's (2002) four lenses of reflection, Ghaye's (2011) theoretical perspective of reflection, Schon's (1991) levels of reflection and the experiential learning cycle of Kolb (1984). These models of reflection will encourage you to see your experiences from a variety of viewpoints, help transform your practice and scaffold your skills in the art of reflection. Like all skills, reflection needs practice; therefore the more you engage in the process of reflection the more proficient and accomplished you will become.

Brookfield's four lenses of reflection

Brookfield (2002) likened critical reflection to the questioning of assumptions related to teaching and learning using four critically reflective lenses:

Lens 1 – through your autobiographical experience;

Lens 2 – through the pupils' eyes;

Lens 3 – through colleagues' perceptions and experiences;

Lens 4 – through theoretical literature.

Critical reflection is not solely about your own reflection on your practice but your consideration and interpretation of other perspectives and viewpoints around you. Viewing your practice through these four lenses will help you to make more informed judgements and to take more informed action. So what does this mean to you as a trainee teacher?

Let us take, for example, the story of *The Very Hungry Caterpillar* (Carle, 2002) as our starting point. We can view the story from a range of perspectives (lenses).

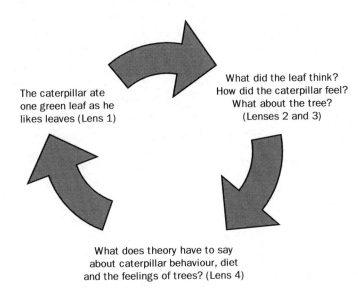

The caterpillar ate one green leaf as he likes leaves (Lens 1)

What did the leaf think? How did the caterpillar feel? What about the tree? (Lenses 2 and 3)

What does theory have to say about caterpillar behaviour, diet and the feelings of trees? (Lens 4)

Figure 1.1 *The Very Hungry Caterpillar through four lenses of reflection (with acknowledgement to Kelly-Freer and Bingle, 2011).*

For those of you who know the story, it is told from the caterpillar's perspective, but what if we were to employ Brookfield's lenses of reflection? You begin to see that previous learning (or in this case past 'eating' experiences) informs the caterpillar and its reasons for plumping for a leaf. Reflection on other perspectives, for example that of the leaf or tree, prompts further consideration and challenges assumptions that it was all right for the caterpillar to eat the leaf, but how does this relate to research and literature surrounding caterpillars' behaviour and diet? This simplistic example should help you to interrogate your own assumptions related to your own and other colleagues' practice and not just to assume that what you observe in school classrooms among even experienced practitioners is always best practice.

Read the scenario below, which recounts one trainee teacher's story about an experience on their school placement. Then complete the table considering each of the four lenses of reflection.

CASE STUDY

George's story

While I was on placement I was using the class teacher's aiming high sheets for setting pupil targets. In my third week of placement I sensed that there were too many targets on the target sheet. The number requiring completion prior to the child receiving an award was unrealistic. They needed to complete ten targets in a term to warrant a reward! From personal experience on this course I know that with too many targets to achieve you disengage and lose the motivation of pupils as the task seems insurmountable. I felt that the children were in a similar position and many did not even know what their targets were. I asked the class teacher sensitively how effective she thought the target setting sheets were, as I was conscious that the class teacher may have designed them. It came to light that the class teacher also thought the target sheets were unwieldy for the children and onerous for staff. We agreed to change the target sheets so that rewards were more easily achievable and children could engage more autonomously. Towards the end of my placement I could see that children were more interested in their targets as a reward was easier to obtain; however, they were still not engaging with the target sheets and I wondered why this might be.

Self / George	Children
Colleagues	Theory

Critical questions

» In light of the case study, complete the table above for each of the four lenses.

» What else could George have done in practice to inform his reflection?

» What other questions would you have asked and who would you have addressed these to?

» What sort of literature and relevant statutory documents would you have considered? How could you improve on the reflection in the scenario?

» Try to rewrite the reflection based on the additional information you potentially could have gained if you had used the four lenses of reflection while in the above situation.

Comment on George's story

While George reflected upon the children's perspectives this could have been further enhanced by a discussion with some of the children to ascertain their views about the target setting system. Likewise, had George consulted statutory guidance on best practice in sharing targets with children, the subsequent design of a target-setting resource would have been further informed. In order for you to develop a rationale for your practice, critical reflection using all four lenses will enable you to reframe any assumptions you have about teaching and learning and potentially save you time in the long run. Therefore, like Brookfield (2002), you may begin to see that critical reflection is vital for your health and well-being as a teacher and for your professional competency in the classroom.

Ghaye's theoretical perspective of reflection

Ghaye (1998) advocates a model of reflection on practice that has at its heart four main emphases, those of reflection on:

*   context;
*   values;
*   improvement;
*   practice.

Underpinning each of the four themes are three key concepts (as seen in Figure 1.2). So how can this model help you to reflect? The following case study describes a situation that a trainee teacher found themselves in during their final placement.

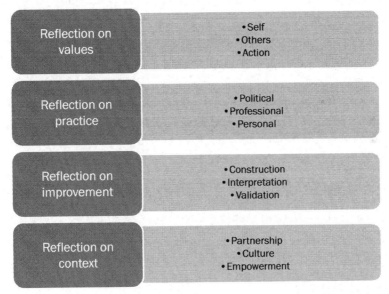

Figure 1.2 *The key concepts underpinning Ghaye's (1998) model of reflection.*

CASE STUDY

Sally's conflict: values versus practice and context

My course had prepared me in readiness for my final placement and I realised that I would be taking more responsibility for the class. I was asked by the class teacher to set reading and mathematics homework each day and a significant task at the end of the week for the Year 2 class. As I regarded homework to be very important I ensured that the children took their reading books home every night and that I reiterated that they needed to practise their times table in readiness for their test at the end of the week. I had never called into question the setting of homework before; however, this was soon to change. The children who had poor results in their times table tests were required to stay in and practise them at lunchtime; an expectation of the school. I was confronted with a parent the following week with a very upset child. The parent explained to me how their home life had been turned upside down due to their partner leaving the family home. This incident made me call into question my values, the need to set the issue in a context which would inform my practice and to find ways I could bring about change. It was not a small feat as I was working within the constraints of the school's expectations but a resolution was desirable as I did not want this type of situation to be repeated.

Using Ghaye's model, consider each of the key ideas in turn to aid the reflection process, along with the critical questions below. Continually asking questions of yourself, about your values and your practice, will become instinctive as you develop your reflective skills.

Critical questions

» What did Sally value at the outset? (Consider the values strand of the model.)

» What might have informed her values initially? (Consider the three key ideas underpinning the reflection on practice concepts.)

» From the scenario, how might the context have influenced Sally? (Consider the context section of the model.)

» How could the information gathered from the above questions improve Sally's thinking in relation to setting homework and any resulting sanctions? (Here you will need to think about how you believe Sally could co-construct and interpret new knowledge to empower her to make changes.)

Extended thinking

» In what ways does reflective theory relate to your practice?

» What strategies do you have for improving your reflective practice throughout your training and in to your future career?

Levels of reflection

Among others, Schon (1991) has been influential in describing levels of reflection and this section is informed by his research.

Reflection *in* practice

Your ability to reflect in practice is crucial to you developing as a skilful reflective classroom practitioner. Throughout your training to become a qualified teacher, you will be asked on numerous occasions to look back on your practice to analyse a situation and if necessary suggest a solution or action to improve your future practice. Nevertheless there will be occasions when time dictates that the act of reflection will need to be more immediate, with quick consequential action. Consider the following case study.

CASE STUDY

Michael's practice

Michael is being observed teaching a mathematics lesson. The teaching input is fast paced and lively. Michael sets the multiplication task with the class and the children move to their seats to begin work on their individual and group tasks. Michael circulates around the class offering support and soon finds that he is surrounded by children out of their seats. It is clear at this point to Michael that the children have not grasped the strategy they should be using to answer the calculations. Michael directs the children back to their seats and says he will get to them as soon as possible but at the moment he is busy working with other children.

Critical questions

» What would you do in this situation? Would you do anything differently?

» How would you justify your actions?

» How could the trainee teacher have used the situation to inform their reflections?

» What obstacles are there for trainee teachers in using reflection 'in' action?

This scenario is not unusual among trainee teachers, or for that matter less experienced class teachers. It nevertheless presents an inner conflict for the trainee. The lesson is obviously not working as the children have not understood the strategy. Faced with this situation, reflection in action should result in quick action, stopping the lesson, re-teaching the strategy and working as a whole class.

Critical questions

» How might you justify moving away from your planning?

» Why do you think trainees are reluctant to stop lessons in this way?

» Would there be any benefits to continuing with the lesson?

» What are the benefits of stopping the lesson and reconvening the class?

Comment on Michael's case study

Continuing with a lesson that is not going well only serves to demonstrate that Michael is not using reflection to inform his practice and he is unable to action effective and necessary change while in the throes of teaching. Worse still, the children in his charge are not learning. He is probably conscious that someone is observing him, he is aware that he has spent a copious amount of time on his planning and therefore stopping the lesson will be viewed as a failure. Quite the reverse is true! By bringing the lesson to a halt and resuming whole-class teaching to address the difficulties and misconceptions, he would demonstrate his reflexive prowess and ability to be adaptable and flexible, but most importantly he would have given the children another chance to learn.

It is a reasonable expectation that you will constantly reflect on the whys and wherefores of your teaching while in the thick of teaching a lesson, relentlessly searching for alternatives and preparing to switch courses at any given moment.

Reflection *on* practice

The mainstay of teacher reflection is the ability to reflect on practice. This generally occurs after a lesson when you look back and consider the pros and cons. You should be mindful however that you do not simply end up back where you started, and you are advised to consider Ghaye's (1998) model which highlights that reflection on practice should be: cyclical, flexible, focused and holistic.

*   Cyclical – reflection *on* practice leads to new and altered cycles of reflection.

*   Flexible – as learning is not linear, you may find you learn something from your practice which means you have to revisit your values and belief systems.

*   Focused – remain focused, identify a direction for your personal development in order to move your practice forward.

*   Holistic – it helps to see learning and teaching as holistic, linked to professional practice, your values and professional development.

You will receive throughout your teaching career opposing viewpoints on how to teach a particular subject effectively, which can be very confusing, and your developmental needs will be very different to someone who is more concerned with relationship building, for example. At this point you might want to consider how you will cope with opposing advice. To summarise Ghaye (1998), learning, teaching and reflection cannot operate in a void and all facets of the model outlined above interrelate and work together to bring about progression in your thinking and practice.

Your involvement with reflection on practice is likely to take many forms. These may include professional dialogue, formal evaluations of your lessons, reflective journals and reflective informed planning, to name but a few.

Professional dialogue

Professional dialogue is a conversation that occurs between two professionals, you as the trainee teacher and perhaps your mentor, classroom teacher or your supervisory tutor. Professional dialogue sits nicely in two of the four lenses of reflection (Brookfield, 2002), that of reflection through colleagues' perceptions and experiences and your own autobiographical experiences. Often professional dialogue will arise following a lesson observation but this is not always the case. Professional dialogue will be ubiquitous on placement. You will encounter it in the staffroom, with parents, among office staff and in interactions with teaching and non-teaching professionals. Each of these discourses should be viewed as an opportunity to challenge your beliefs and assumptions and inform your knowledge and understanding related to teaching in its broadest sense. At its most poignant is the professional discourse that takes place between you and your class teacher, mentor or tutor following a lesson observation. The way in which you engage in this professional conversation is crucial in terms of your professional development.

Critical question

» *Try to think of an occasion when you have had a professional dialogue. This might be with a mentor in school, a university tutor or a fellow trainee on your course. From your own experience, examine the dialogue and reflect on which model of reflection would have aided your reflection.*

Using video

The reflection process can be aided by using video. Understandably many trainee teachers are reticent to have themselves recorded on video. For many of us it is often a painful experience to watch ourselves; however, the use of video is a powerful vehicle with which you can improve your practice. Think about the following real-life scenario.

CASE STUDY

Marta's story

I was reflecting on my lesson which had gone particularly well and I thought there was little I could improve on. When my mentor told me that during the PE lesson I could not see all the children at any given point in time, I was a little bemused. I was sure that I had been circulating around the class and became quite defensive in response to her observation. At this point my mentor asked if she could video my next PE lesson so that we might look at it together and did not pursue the point any further. I was rather reluctant to be videoed, but just like any other observation once I had started to teach I forgot that the camera was there. Then it was time to get my feedback. Once again I felt the lesson was good, which the mentor agreed with, but still the issue of seeing all the children throughout the entire lesson came to the fore. I started to contradict the point the mentor was making at which point she suggested we viewed the video footage from the lesson. Oh my word, while it was embarrassing in the first instance watching myself, it highlighted so many nuances in my practice. Firstly the mentor was quite right in her assertion that I was unable to see the entire class throughout the lesson as I had positioned myself in the middle of the hall and half the children were behind me. I had felt that I was circulating, which was true, but a joint understanding based on each of our reflections was lacking. Secondly I noticed that I kept saying 'like' and 'kinda' when explaining instructions to the class.

Critical questions

» *In what ways did the videoing help Marta to reflect?*

» *What lenses of reflection did she employ?*

»   *What would be your reaction if you were asked by your mentor for permission to video you while teaching?*

»   *What other benefits might there be in the use of video?*

An additional benefit of the use of video is the opportunity to assess children. On many occasions the replaying of video footage can highlight children's responses, or in the case of PE flag those children who have performed over expectations or those that need further support. It is a powerful tool therefore not only in your own professional development but also in the learning and development of the children in your charge.

Using a reflective journal

When you are in your school placement you will find that you have extensive occasions to make entries in your reflective journal. Records in this journal should not purely regurgitate what you did but should demonstrate the nature and extent of your ability to reflect, review your attributes and your professional behaviour. You will be trying to make sense of observations and diverse ideas as well as wrestling with your own values in an effort to make sense of the teaching world you are now hopefully immersed in. In a bid to reassure you, your journal entries should be succinct and to the point. They should clarify the context but ultimately demonstrate what you have learnt from the experience. You do not need to write a chronicle of events! You may find that reflective journals are often referred to as professional development profiles (PDPs) depending on your initial teacher training provider.

Using the knowledge you have gained from this chapter and your wider reading, critically evaluate the two entries below from different reflective journals. You may also like to read Moon's (2006) work, which goes into greater detail about reflection and maps the process. This will aid your reflective writing skills significantly.

CASE STUDY

Reflective journal entry 1

During a PE lesson on the field, I was sure to set clear boundaries for the children as to where they could go. This enabled me to keep the class safe as I was able to see all of the children.

Reflective journal entry 2

I am becoming increasingly aware of how to develop effective communication with colleagues, more specifically teaching assistants (TAs) and support staff. I appreciate that these additional adults in the classroom need to have an overview of what I am trying to achieve and why. At the start of the day I make time to talk to TAs to ensure they are aware of what is needed from them. I have also started writing this out for TAs to refer to in the lesson – ensuring that the learning objectives are understood and are more likely to be achieved. From doing this I have learnt the importance of effective communication, however I now need to think about how I will manage this if I have to do this for more lessons and need to discuss this with my mentor and the TAs. I have also made a point of letting the children know who they can go to if they need help. The children appear to spend more time on task now instead of walking around the classroom trying to get my attention.

Your reflective journal is an essential instrument in your development as a teacher. The following questions will help to consolidate what you know about reflective journals.

Critical questions

»   *Which of the two journal entries do you regard as being more reflective?*

»   *Explain your answer with reference to the features each exhibits.*

»   *What is the purpose of completing a reflective journal?*

»   *What are the features of good reflective writing?*

»   *How will you ensure that your journal entries are reflective rather than descriptive?*

»   *What types of high-quality evidence are you considering using?*

You will be expected to gather high-quality evidence to support your reflective entries. Further guidance as to what constitutes high-quality evidence will be disseminated by your training provider. You may also like to refer to Blatchford (2012), who applies the Teachers' Standards to the practicalities of the classroom.

Reflection *for* action

In order to inform yourself you will find observing other professionals beneficial. These observations will inform what actions you might need to take and be appropriate in relation to your practice. A word of warning, however, is needed so that you approach these observations objectively and sensitively. Another fellow professional will have invited or agreed for you to observe their practice. Ideally you should agree or at least inform them of your focus. For example, you might want to develop your assessment for learning strategies. If this is the case then you should look for what strategies the teacher employs. It is very easy to highlight the shortcomings of someone's practice even if they are experienced; however, do bear in mind that you are the trainee in this relationship. If you keep reflective notes consider whether you would be happy to share them with the individual you have just observed. If the answer to this is yes, then you have retained your professional integrity and not compromised your position with the staff in school generally.

Reflection *on* action

Finally in this section related to the levels of reflection, you should consider what you have actioned and whether it was successful. If it was unsuccessful then you need to initiate a whole new cycle of reflection; Kolb's model (see below) may assist you in this learning process. You may also want to consider how your action has informed your planning, teaching and the subsequent learning of the pupils in your charge. Significantly, have your pupils made progress? Have you improved your practice in relation to the teaching standards?

The reflective practitioner

Reflective practitioners not only reflect on their own practice but on the practice of others in order to inform their personal and professional development. You will be expected to

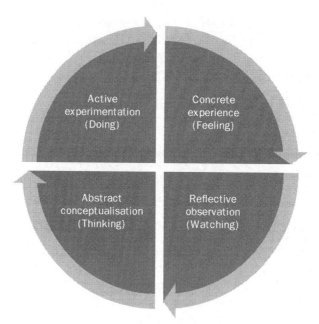

Figure 1.3 *Kolb's (1984) experiential learning cycle.*

take on board many different and opposing perspectives in a confusing world and make sense of those perspectives so as to organise your next steps. Kolb's experiential learning cycle (Figure 1.3) helps us to see the reflection process more succinctly, to consider the ambiguities surrounding teaching and learning and to try to structure the chaos surrounding our developing practice.

It is exceedingly important that you take ownership of your developmental journey. Whilst it is easy to have someone tell you what to work on next, it is more empowering and rewarding if you can evaluate your own practice in a bid to be a reflective practitioner who can critically reflect so as to move their teacher training and career forward. You should be able to move from being told what is going well and not so well to a point where you can identify the aspects of your practice that are good and you utilise to the full, down to the points that you have identified as in need of further development. You should be able to set your own targets for further development rather than rely on others to tell you what you need to develop.

Critical questions

»   Consider again the Teachers' Standards referred to at the beginning of the chapter (page 5).

»   Explain how reflection throughout practice relates to each of these Teachers' Standards.

»   How does assessment of pupils fit into the reflection cycle?

Chapter reflections

If you arm yourself with the right tools for reflection, potentially you have the ability to transform your practice. Failure to gain the skills to reflect critically on your practice will in turn impact on your ability to be a teacher of high quality and potentially become a barrier to you realising any dream of being an 'outstanding' teacher.

Critical points

» *Look inwardly and outwardly in order to inform reflection.*

» *Be open to other individuals' diverse and contrary opinions and perspectives.*

» *Practise your reflective writing skills.*

» *Remember to reflect not regurgitate!*

» *Develop your ability to be self-reflective and set your own targets.*

Taking it further

Cooperrider, D L and Whitney, D (2005) *Appreciative Inquiry: A Positive Revolution in Change*. San Francisco, CA: Berrett-Koehler Publishers.

Griffin, M (2003) Using Critical Incidents to Promote and Assess Reflective Thinking in Preservice Teachers. *Reflective Practice*, 4 (2), 207–220.

Hobbs, V (2007) Faking it or Hating it: Can Reflective Practice be Forced? *Reflective Practice*, 8(3), pp.405–417.

Jay, J K and Johnson, K L (2002) Capturing Complexity: A Typology of Reflective Practice for Teacher Education. *Teaching and Teacher Education*, 18, 73–85.

Loughran, J, (2002) Effective Reflective Practice: In Search of Meaning in Learning about Teaching. *Journal of Teacher Education*, 53 (1), 33–43.

Moon, J A (2006) (2nd edn) *Learning Journals: A Handbook for Reflective Practice and Professional Development*. Abingdon: Routledge.

2 Individual professional attributes

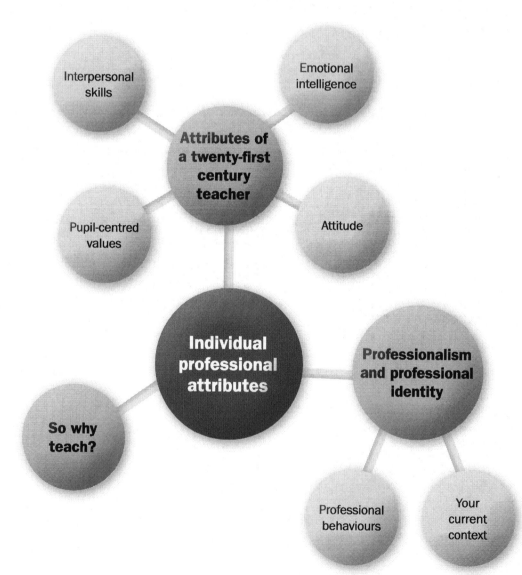

Interpersonal skills

Emotional intelligence

Attributes of a twenty-first century teacher

Pupil-centred values

Attitude

Individual professional attributes

Professionalism and professional identity

So why teach?

Professional behaviours

Your current context

Teachers' Standards (DfE, 2011c)

PART TWO: PERSONAL AND PROFESSIONAL CONDUCT

A teacher is expected to demonstrate consistently high standards of personal and professional conduct. The following statements define the behaviour and attitudes which set the required standard for conduct throughout a teacher's career.

- Teachers uphold public trust in the profession and maintain high standards of ethics and behaviour, within and outside school, by:
  - treating pupils with dignity, building relationships rooted in mutual respect, and at all times observing proper boundaries appropriate to a teacher's professional position;
  - having regard for the need to safeguard pupils' well-being, in accordance with statutory provisions;
  - showing tolerance of and respect for the rights of others;
  - not undermining fundamental British values, including democracy, the rule of law, individual liberty and mutual respect, and tolerance of those with different faiths and beliefs;
  - ensuring that personal beliefs are not expressed in ways which exploit pupils' vulnerability or might lead them to break the law.
- Teachers must have proper and professional regard for the ethos, policies and practices of the school in which they teach, and maintain high standards in their own attendance and punctuality.
- Teachers must have an understanding of, and always act within, the statutory frameworks which set out their professional duties and responsibilities.

Introduction

Teaching is a career that provides opportunities, challenges and individual reward through the inspiration of pupils to achieve their goal. The ability to stimulate young people to learn means that you have to possess certain qualities and attributes and demonstrate certain behaviours. These qualities are not an exact science; however, this chapter provides some examples of the types of qualities, skills and knowledge a teacher should hold. The personal and professional code outlined above is of great importance while training as a teacher, throughout your future teaching career and even on your very first visit to a placement school. Underpinning the professional and personal conduct are Teachers' Standards 1–8 (DfE, 2011c). Collectively they provide a benchmark for the individual attributes desirable in a teacher. Meeting the standards is the minimum required of you. This chapter highlights the values and attributes desirable in a developing teaching professional in the twenty-first century. Some, if not all, of these attributes you will already exhibit, having been selected for a teacher training course. There may be others that you need to develop. The chapter will focus on the attitudes of the best teachers and certain behaviours they exhibit with the intention that, with reflection, you will become more self-aware. A range of professional attributes is considered and a self-audit is provided so that you can examine your strengths in each of these areas.

Attributes of a twenty-first century teacher

Pupil-centred values

So why have you decided to become a teacher? One would hope that it is down to your passion for working with children. Your past experiences probably informed your career choice and you recognised that you like children, want to make a difference and revel in their light bulb moments! If this sounds like you, then you have made a wise career choice. You may be surprised to know that not all teachers hold such core values or attitudes towards children. A key attribute of being a successful teacher in the twenty-first century is having a pupil-centred value system. The voice of the child is paramount in terms of education in its broadest sense, for example it informs the presence of a school council. In addition, valuing the pupil's voice on a day-to-day basis in relation to their learning is key to providing a personalised learning experience for all children. How can you provide an effective tailored education for all pupils without listening to the preferences they have in terms of what they would like to learn? Are you and the pupils equal in your classroom? Or do you see yourself as the boss, the font of all knowledge, the expert that imparts this knowledge into compliant individuals? Intrinsically you should have a belief that all children can learn, no matter what their culture, background or specific need may be. Likewise if you are child-centred you will no doubt have a commitment to nurturing the potential in each and every pupil. The value and importance you place on the pupils, and how you view them, is core to any good teacher.

Interpersonal skills

From the time you were interviewed, your interpersonal skills will have been under scrutiny. For example, in taught sessions at your college or university your tutors will be assessing your ability to engage, be a team player and form positive relationships with your peers and staff. These skills will play a key role while you are on your teaching placement and in your future career as a teacher. Your ability, for example, to establish professional relationships with colleagues, pupils and parents (Teachers' Standard 8, DfE, 2011c) will be fundamental to your success on placement. You may naturally be a quiet, more retiring individual but you will still need to be proactive in establishing effective relationships as promptly as possible when you enter your placement. Some trainee teachers make the mistake of thinking that you need to be friends with those in your placement school, including the pupils. This is a myth and you are well advised to avoid this wherever possible. Remember that you are being assessed by your mentor and you are going to be the pupils' teacher, and as such you need to maintain professional boundaries and relationships in order to deliver as a class teacher.

In addition you need to be highly organised, a good timekeeper, honest and have high levels of integrity in order to perform your duties as a trainee teacher to the highest degree. You are being placed in a position of trust while on placement and as such should work to gain the trust of all those in your placement setting. Abusing trust or failing to meet the high expectations placed upon you in any of the areas mentioned above will inevitably lead to a difficult situation and potentially, in worst-case scenarios, termination of your placement.

Your ability to be adaptable and flexible will be tested to the maximum while on placement. Life in a primary school is not without its idiosyncrasies and you will frequently find yourself in changing circumstances. These may be on a daily basis due to timetabling changes but could involve national change due to political interference, for example the imminent changes to the national curriculum. Read Shahnaze's account of her experience when teaching for the first time in her placement school.

CASE STUDY

Shahnaze's story

I was really excited about my first full week of teaching. I had spent the weekend planning and had prepared all the resources I would need for my first day. I had feedback from my mentor in relation to my plans and had adapted them in the light of his feedback. I was really well prepared and eager to get started. Prior to commencing my first lesson, my mentor said that there was a visitor from a local charity coming to talk at the morning assembly. The assembly would therefore start earlier than usual. I was quite agitated as I had spent all that time planning and even when the mentor gave me feedback on my planning he did not mention anything. Why had no one told me earlier? I would not have planned so much if I had known. I realised that I would lose about 15 minutes of my planned lesson but thought it would be fine; how wrong could I be? The time just flew by. I didn't know what to cut out of the lesson or how to fit everything in. I ended up cutting the lesson short so that the children could tidy up the classroom before they were led into assembly, and even then my class was the last to arrive in the hall.

My next lesson was mathematics and once more I was fully prepared. The children had gone from assembly straight out to play and I was waiting in anticipation for their arrival. I waited and I waited and there was no sign of them. The pupils were almost ten minutes late coming in because they had been granted extra playtime because they had sat so long in the hall listening to the visitor! How utterly ridiculous! I thought educating children was the most important agenda for a school – not having extended playtimes and sitting in assembly? Once more my lesson had been disrupted; no one had told me that the children would be outside for longer than usual. This resulted in me not being able to cover all that was on my plan. I was so frustrated and just wanted to throw in the towel. I had spent so long on my planning and all for nothing; a waste of my time and energy.

Critical questions

»   If you were in Shahnaze's shoes, what would you have done to be better prepared for the lesson disruptions?

»   What is your view of extended playtimes and assemblies? What are their purposes in terms of educating pupils?

»   How do you perceive Shahnaze's view of education? How are your views similar or different? Why?

» How would you adapt your lessons so as to fit the time available?

» How do you think you might feel if you have to cut short your lessons? How would you manage these feelings?

» How resilient do you believe Shahnaze is? If faced with the same situation, have you considered how resilient you might be? What strategies could you put in place to ensure that you maintain your resilience levels?

Comment on Shahnaze's story

Shahnaze had clearly worked hard to prepare for her week of teaching as her plans had been written and commented upon ahead of time. In the first instance, however, Shahnaze was not proactive in her approach. Routinely at the start of the day Shahnaze should have consulted with her mentor to find out if there were any special circumstances that day: changes to the timetable required to accommodate unusual events such as longer assemblies, pupil photograph days or even pupils coming in and out because of peripatetic music lessons. Having ascertained what anomalies there were to the school day, Shahnaze would then have been in a position to ask for the mentor's advice as to what might be sensible to leave out of the lesson or which parts to cut short. Alternatively she could have asked the mentor the previous week what events were scheduled for the forthcoming week and then planned accordingly. In addition one would have to ask why Shahnaze did not go out and check why the children were late in from playtime. Likewise why was she not in attendance at the assembly to hear the message about an extended playtime? Again this would have given her time to check with the mentor on how she might adapt her lesson.

Shahnaze's attitude towards assembly and playtime is an interesting one. Pupils' holistic development should be central to all educators; it is not sufficient to merely address the national curriculum at primary school level. You should be providing opportunities for children to develop their social skills such as turn-taking and interactions when engaged in play. In the case of Shahnaze's class, the children needed a wake-up and shake-up having sat for a long period of time in the hall. The pupils' concentration (had they gone straight into their maths lesson) would have been significantly marred so an appropriate break time was required.

Assembly is another opportunity for children to engage in the wider curriculum and provides scope for citizenship education through community cohesion; all valuable learning contexts for young children. Finally it should be noted that Shahnaze demonstrated limited (if any) reflective skills. Her aptitude to continually strive towards excellence and improve her practice appears lacking even though she had all her plans prepared. In addition she appeared to lack resilience when faced with a set-back due to feeling that she had wasted her time and energy planning for no apparent reason. If Shahnaze had taken more responsibility for the class and enquired at an earlier stage, the situation would never have arisen.

Extended thinking

» What is resilience?

» How can you foster resilience?

» *Why might resilience be an issue in education?*

» *If you would like to learn more about developing approaches to resilience, please refer to Day et al. (2011)*

Emotional intelligence

As a primary school teacher you should have empathy not only for those that you teach but also for colleagues you work with. You need to consider your ability to sense whether pupils or indeed colleagues might be having a difficult time. In terms of pupils this is crucial when considering aspects of child protection, for instance. This innate ability may come more naturally to some than to others; however, one key attribute that you can develop in order to enhance your emotional intelligence is your ability to listen for meaning. You are more likely to be sensitive if meaning has been established between you and the person conveying the message.

You will also need to be a master of managing your own emotions. This is crucial as there will be times when you are placed in stressful situations and you will be expected to deal with them without getting angry, finding a solution calmly and professionally. You may find this a challenge so you will need to consider developing strategies that you can implement in order to address any shortcomings in this area and regulate your emotions. If you master this element of your personality you will be more competent in effectively managing relationships with pupils, parents and colleagues. Likewise those with a high degree of emotional intelligence will know themselves well, react positively to constructive criticism and achieve highly. In summary, if you have high levels of emotional intelligence you will invariably exhibit the following personal characteristics:

*   self-awareness;
*   self-regulation;
*   motivation;
*   excellent social skills.

The good news is that you can be taught how to develop your emotional intelligence. Consider the following critical questions to establish your levels of emotional intelligence.

Critical questions

» *How do you react to people? Are you quick to judge?*

» *How open and accepting are you to alternative perspectives?*

» *How intuitive are you to other people's feelings?*

» *How good are you at listening to others? How do you know?*

» *When listening, do you start to think about what you are going to say next in response?*

» *How do you react in stressful situations?*

» *How often do you blame others or get angry with them?*

» *How easy do you find it to make an honest apology for your actions if they negatively impact on individuals?*

» *How do your actions impact on others?*

» *In what areas could you further develop your emotional intelligence?*

Extended thinking

» *Why is emotional intelligence important? Explain your answer as fully as you can.*

If you feel this is an area that you need to develop, or you wish to promote emotional intelligence with your pupils, the Taking it further section at the end of the chapter provides some suggestions.

Attitude

In order to enthuse the children in your class, you will need to have a positive and passionate attitude towards them and towards all of the curriculum subjects you teach in order to lead learning. You may find that you struggle with some subjects and these need to be the ones on which you spend the longest time planning and preparing. The Teacher Development Agency ((TDA) as it was known at the time) produced helpful guidance in 2007 to support trainee teachers in their continuing professional development (CPD), particularly in terms of subject knowledge. They considered that your attitude towards a subject could significantly influence the progress you made as a developing practitioner. The guidance circulated by the TDA (2007) outlined five key areas connected with attitudes that developing professionals need to be mindful of when planning and teaching lessons. You need to consider your attitude towards:

- inclusion, achievement and well-being of all pupils;

- the subject or the curriculum area and enthusiasm for teaching it;

- being creative in developing learning opportunities for all pupils;

- continuing professional development within the subject or curriculum area;

- working as part of a team, learning from others and contributing to the learning community.

In light of the five key indicators for attitude mentioned above, consider the following account of Adrian's first attempt at teaching music.

CASE STUDY

Adrian's music lesson

I must admit that I'm not very good at music. I have little subject knowledge, just the bits I picked up on my training course. Reading music is like reading a foreign language! I can't play an instrument and as for singing I really lack confidence. I planned to deliver a music lesson to a Year 2 class. I knew I had a hearing-impaired child in the class and began to question how I could get him involved. In my lesson I got children to sing a song that I had to teach them from the outset. But the response from the children was like pulling teeth! I played the CD to them over and over again but I just didn't seem to be getting anywhere. The child that was hearing-impaired started to disrupt the rest of the class, which was out of character. My mentor said after the lesson that I lacked enthusiasm and confidence. Well what did they expect? I don't really like music but I tried my best.

Critical questions

» How could Adrian plan for and teach his music lesson so that it included all pupils, including the hearing-impaired child?

» In what way could Adrian have been more creative in developing learning opportunities for the Year 2 class?

» Undoubtedly Adrian did not demonstrate engagement with CPD in music or his ability to learn from others. What would you suggest Adrian do in order to improve his subject knowledge in this area?

» How would these suggestions help Adrian with his confidence in and enthusiasm for the subject?

Comment on Adrian's music lesson

Adrian clearly recognised that he struggled in the subject of music but the case study highlights a less than satisfactory attitude to the subject. All pupils are entitled to be taught the national curriculum (DfE, 2013b) subjects effectively. If you have poor subject knowledge, and a lack of confidence and enthusiasm, you need to ensure that you are proactive and seek advice. While you may still find the subject more challenging, you have demonstrated your positive attitude, and your desire to teach well and to do your best.

Professionalism and professional identity

Now that you are a trainee teacher, realistically this is the beginning of your professional career; however, do not underestimate how your sense of professionalism will evolve throughout the duration of the rest of your working life. Already you will have started to construct your own sense of professional identity, ie how you see yourself as a teacher. This sense of growing professionalism will relate to your own personal life history, your training and the type of personality you have. How you see yourself as a teacher is just the start of a teacher's lifetime's journey and your professional identity will continue to evolve until you leave the profession. This view is backed up by a range of research, for example authors such as Day et al. (2006) clearly indicate that as you move through your teaching career your initial zeal for the profession will change and develop as well as grow and diminish. This in turn may have a positive or negative influence upon how you feel with regard to your professional morale, motivation and job satisfaction. This is natural and something that you should not feel worried about. At this stage of your career, despite any worries, you should be highly motivated, keen and eager to succeed. You are likely to be buoyant about the prospect of getting into school and be looking forward to teaching children.

It may be useful to start to see your emerging professional self or emerging sense of professional identity as being related to what Day and Kington (2008) suggest are the personal and situational dimensions of teacher identity. Do not dismiss how your age, health, personal circumstances, where you work and the climate or ethos of the school have influence upon your feelings about teaching. These factors will all impact on your desire to remain in the profession; something often referred to as the levels of retention.

It is helpful to consider some of the issues that you might face not only now but also during your professional career. As someone new to the profession you might find it useful to review the following issues as a means of reflecting on your current professionalism as well as preparing yourself for your professional future.

Your current context

The context in which you are being trained as a teacher will have a major influence upon your sense of professionalism. Your school placements will definitely influence your professional feelings while training. For example, your placement school's facilities, resources, school buildings, culture and ethos will provide you with positive and negative professional feelings. These factors will all mould your sense of professional identity, your levels of motivation, morale, job satisfaction and feelings about the profession. As Day and Gu (2007) rightly point out, the conditions in which teachers work play a vital role in their levels of professional commitment. This is important given that a school's best asset is often seen in terms of its workforce. This research is supported by Howard (2012), who clearly outlines how a change in a school building, its facilities and levels of resourcing can positively influence teachers' feelings regarding doing their job, but also how they can enhance their sense of professional identity, motivation, morale and job satisfaction.

So thinking in terms of your training context you might like to consider the following factors and how they impact upon your sense of professionalism:

- the geographical and school setting in which you work, ie the school's facilities, resources and buildings;
- the staff, governance and pupils;
- the opportunities for professional development;
- the ethos and culture of the school.

Critical questions

» *If you know where you will undertake your school placement, how do you currently feel about the school?*

» *Do the levels of resourcing, the school building and its facilities make you feel positive about teaching or do they frustrate you?*

» *Do you get satisfaction in working in your placement school with your mentor?*

» Does your mentor value you and provide you with opportunities to progress as a professional?

Professional behaviours

The way in which you behave, not only in school but also in public, can have devastating consequences. You therefore need to be mindful of a whole raft of items associated with your personal conduct as well as your professional conduct. Nigel's story, detailed below, outlines an incident that happened while he was on his PGCE course.

CASE STUDY

Nigel's story

I was on a night out with my mates and we hit town at the normal time and went to a few pubs. I wasn't on school placement and it was a Friday night so I didn't have to worry about getting up for university the next day. Spirits were running high with a feeling of euphoria as we had all just come to the end of our teacher training course and were celebrating passing our last pieces of academic work and were awaiting our results. All our teaching placements were out of the way so it was time to let our hair down. Well things got a bit raucous and we continued to drink, boys larking around really. We left the pub and I was playing the fool. Someone in the group said something and I exposed my behind! At that moment a police car drove by. They arrested me on the spot and took me to the police station. I was shocked that I had been arrested for what I thought was a minor incident but didn't know at that point the seriousness of my actions. The police even contacted my teacher training college. They do that, you know!

Critical questions

» What parts of the personal and professional codes of conduct did Nigel contravene?

» What consequences would result from Nigel's actions?

» How could Nigel have avoided the vulnerable position in which he found himself?

Comment on Nigel's story

Many aspects of personal and professional conduct were breached on Nigel's night out. He clearly did not have due regard for maintaining high personal standards of behaviour or mutual respect for others, and did not observe the boundaries placed upon him as a teacher. He flaunted safeguarding guidance and committed an unlawful act. Teacher training providers, when confronted with this situation, would initiate a full investigation based on the evidence presented by the accused. Due to the nature of this offence, an independent safeguarding committee at the teacher training provider and/or a 'Fitness to Teach' committee would hear the case. Nigel's offence was serious enough for him to be registered on the barred list for working with children. This was a life-long sentence for Nigel who had spent a year training on his PGCE course to reach his ultimate goal of being a primary school teacher. While his dream had been within reach, it was shattered through one ill-conceived act on a night out.

Table 2.1 *Personal and professional self-evaluation tool*

Personal and professional conduct	Evidence	Developmental targets
Do you treat pupils (and others) with dignity?		
Do you maintain high ethical standards?		
Do you maintain high standards of behaviour at all times?		
Do you have mutual respect for all?		
Do you observe boundaries appropriate to a teacher's position?		
Do you safeguard pupils' well-being?		
Do you tolerate and have respect for the rights of others?		
Do you uphold fundamental British values?		
Are you democratic?		
Do you abide by the law?		
Do you uphold individual liberty?		
Do you tolerate different faiths and beliefs?		
Are you mindful of personal beliefs and how these may impact on pupils?		
Do you have due regard for the ethos, policies and practice of the school?		
Do you maintain high standards of attendance?		
Do you maintain high standards of punctuality?		
Do you understand and work within the statutory frameworks for teachers?		

Extended thinking

» What are the main professional attributes teachers should possess?

» How will you demonstrate these in your practice and through the teaching of pupils in your class?

» How would you tackle extremism if faced with this issue?

In order to complete the self-audit table above you may have to consider your behaviours in light of your past personal and professional experiences and especially if you have limited experience of working with pupils. For example, consider your conduct on a night out. Is your behaviour always of the highest standard? If not, what do you intend to do about it? What development target will you set for yourself? For this self-evaluation tool to effect positive change in your conduct, you will need to be completely honest with yourself.

So why teach?

Given that personal and context-specific factors will mould your sense of professional identity, it is important to remember that most trainee teachers, and no doubt yourself, enter into teaching to make a difference, see pupils develop and work with colleagues. These are items that researchers such as Dinham and Scott (1998, 2000) suggest are the 'intrinsic satisfiers' of teaching. For other researchers, such as Scott et al. (1999), motivation of teachers is linked to their altruism, affiliation and personal growth. However, whatever your level of motivation and commitment it is important that you recognise that extrinsic factors to the school environment such as levels of pay, the pace of continual change and initiative overload will at times prove a challenge to your positive feelings for wanting to be a teacher. This again is normal for everyone in the profession, so do not worry. Keep remembering that you are making a difference to young children's lives. You provide the emotional rock for many, a constant in their ever-changing lives, a source of inspiration and comfort. You may have had a teacher who made a difference to your life. It is now your chance to offer a child this wonderful gift.

Chapter reflections

While some attributes desirable in a trainee teacher may come naturally to you, others may not. This is not the end of the world if you have a strong desire to succeed and want to resolve the situation. Personal and professional competencies can be developed. For you to shine as an outstanding trainee you will need to take control, dedicate personal time and effort to nurturing these competencies, and as a result your teaching persona will be significantly enhanced.

Critical points

»   *Children should be central to your value system.*

»   *Be proactive in developing relationships.*

»   *Honesty, trust and the highest personal and professional standards are expected both inside and outside the classroom.*

»   *Resilience is crucial if you are going to survive in the teaching profession.*

»   *Wider factors such as school buildings can impact on your personal and professional conduct. Think about these when you apply for your first job!*

»   *Be honest with yourself about your strengths and weaknesses in this area and make efforts to develop the professional competencies.*

»   *Stay true to your desire to become a teacher.*

Taking it further

Colverd, S and Hodgkin, B (2011) *Developing Emotional Intelligence in the Primary School.* Abingdon: Routledge.

Corcoran, R and Torney, R (2012) *Developing Emotionally Competent Teachers: Emotional Intelligence and Pre-service Teacher Education.* www.peterlang.com/.

3 Placement practicalities

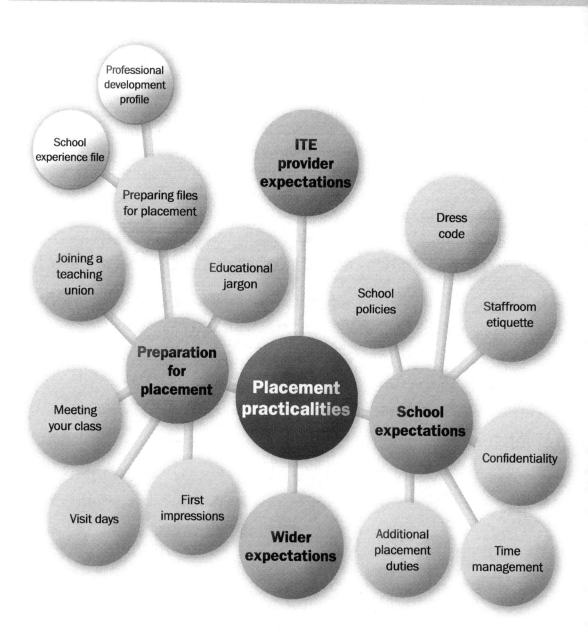

Teachers' Standards (DfE, 2011c)

1 Set high expectations which inspire, motivate and challenge pupils

- establish a safe and stimulating environment for pupils, rooted in mutual respect
- demonstrate consistently the positive attitudes, values and behaviour which are expected of pupils.

7 Manage behaviour effectively to ensure a good and safe learning environment

- have clear rules and routines for behaviour in classrooms, and take responsibility for promoting good and courteous behaviour both in classrooms and around the school, in accordance with the school's behaviour policy
- have high expectations of behaviour, and establish a framework for discipline with a range of strategies, using praise, sanctions and rewards consistently and fairly
- maintain good relationships with pupils, exercise appropriate authority, and act decisively when necessary.

8 Fulfil wider professional responsibilities

- make a positive contribution to the wider life and ethos of the school
- develop effective professional relationships with colleagues, knowing how and when to draw on advice and specialist support.

Introduction

This is probably the moment that you have been waiting for – your school placement. You are likely to feel excited but equally you may feel quite daunted by the prospect. This chapter seeks to appease your feelings of apprehension in order to best prepare you for what lies ahead. It gives guidance on what to expect on your school placement, and presents case studies so that you can exercise your developing critical reflective skills and subsequently change your actions if needed.

From the outset you will be expected to demonstrate consistently high standards of personal and professional conduct in keeping with Part Two of the Teachers' Standards (DfE, 2012f). This code of conduct underpins the standard of behaviour and attitude expected from you as a teacher in and out of school. You will be required to live by this code in order to achieve the standard required to be a teacher. We discussed this aspect of your placement in more depth in Chapter 2.

Preparation for placement

First impressions

First impressions really do count! Your ITE provider will invariably find each school placement for you, so once you know where your placement is to be conducted, there are a few basics to get right. In the first instance it is not only customary but courteous to contact the school in order to introduce yourself. This first conversation is usually with the school administrator.

Bear in mind that they will have the ear of the head teacher, and you should count this first conversation as vitally important for setting the right impression. This initial conversation will permit you to confirm arrangements for your placement with the school. For example:

- What time does school start?
- What time would the school like you to arrive?
- Which class are you with? (Sometimes your placement may change at the last minute due to situations in school beyond anyone's control.)
- What is the class teacher called?
- Who should you ask for on your arrival?

Following your introductory telephone call to the school, it is sensible to make a trial journey to the school prior to your first day of placement to check the exact location of the school and approximate time of the journey.

Additionally it is advisable to read the school's prospectus, which can often be viewed on the school website online. The school website will provide you with a clearer picture of the ethos of the school, the staff that work there and what the children have been learning.

Visit days

On occasions ITE providers may facilitate pre-experience visit days so that you can meet your class teacher and the pupils. This visit is very important as it will be the first time that you will have contact with the teacher you will be working with throughout the practice and, equally important, the pupils you will teach. It will also enable you to plan ahead of your placement, including simple but important things like the location of the photocopier and basic school routines. The visit will help you find out what you will be teaching as part of the curriculum, enable you to collect a timetable and begin to organise the first couple of days of your placement. Similarly it provides you with time to find out the roles that certain people play within the setting and what to do in the event of an emergency. It is vital that you get this initial meeting spot on! Remember to remain professional throughout, since a lack of professionalism could potentially have a devastating impact on your placement. The following case study illustrates how important it is for you to conduct yourself from the outset as though you were a fully-fledged teacher.

CASE STUDY

A mentor's experience of a visit day

I was delighted to hear that I had been assigned a trainee teacher, Victoria, and was looking forward to her arrival. When Victoria arrived she was very personable and friendly. Having a new adult in your classroom can be quite daunting so the early signs were good. When break time came, Victoria asked if she could leave at lunchtime. As I had substantial experience of working with trainee teachers and had attended the mentor training event run by the college earlier in the year, I was acutely aware of the expectations placed upon Victoria. I was therefore very surprised by the request. When challenged, Victoria stated that the college had not stipulated she needed to be there all day and therefore she thought she could leave at lunchtime. I told Victoria that my understanding was that she was to remain in school for the whole day. This would allow me to talk to her at lunchtime and after school about the topics she would be teaching. Furthermore I would provide her with information related to the individual needs of the children she would eventually teach. I told Victoria I would check with the college immediately and let her know. At lunchtime I had confirmation from the college that Victoria was expected in school all day and that she had been told this. When I went to find Victoria, I discovered that she had taken herself off into town without informing me. At this point I was disappointed in the level of Victoria's professionalism and dedication. When Victoria returned I asked her to meet with me and outlined my concerns. Victoria listened but did not agree that her conduct was unacceptable. Victoria still insisted that she needed to leave so she could finish an assignment that was due imminently. At this point I reluctantly agreed she could leave the school. As Victoria left the front door I heard some of my children asking Victoria where she was going and she responded by saying that she had to leave because I did not like her. At that point I picked up the phone, rang the college and withdrew Victoria's placement.

Critical questions

» Consider a visit day to your new school placement and list the aims you have for your visit.

» What do you want to achieve by the end of the day?

» What justification did the mentor have in asking Victoria to leave and withdrawing the placement?

» How could Victoria have rectified the situation?

Comment on Victoria's visit

Victoria should have considered the purpose of the visit day, and if she had concerns or queries, these should have been raised with her tutor at college. Generally schools and ITE providers already have a very well-established relationship and they talk to each other regularly. Likewise the teachers working in the partnership schools you will be placed in already know the expectations for your course, as they will have attended training prior to your arrival, been sent school experience expectation information and may well have been trained in the same institution.

Meeting your class

More often than not, the experience of meeting your class for the first time will be an exciting one. Clearly you will want more than anything to make a good impression and your first encounter needs to set the tone and expectations you have for the children. Experience has shown that on occasions trainee teachers are desperate to be liked by the pupils in their class. This is quite understandable as the majority of people do not want to be viewed as a tyrant; however, there is a fine line between being friendly and retaining authority: a balancing act for sure! The pupils in your class are not your friends, they are your educational charges and as such you need to ensure that you set your boundaries from the outset. Overly friendly, and you will find that you will struggle to be viewed as the teacher figure and role model required. Too authoritarian and you risk not being able to build effective relationships which will enable the pupils to learn.

Critical questions

»   *How will you manage this aspect of your teaching practice? What preparation could you do?*

»   *What interpersonal skills will you need to develop when striking the right balance between being a teacher who has good relationships with pupils and one who needs to gain respect?*

Extended thinking

»   *What sort of impression is it important for you to make on your visit days?*

»   *How will you make certain you will present yourself in the best light to the school on your visit?*

Preparing files for placement

School experience file

For each placement that you undertake you will need to set up and maintain certain teaching files. While initially there will be very little in this file, having it ready to take to your first visit sends out a clear professional signal that you are organised, motivated and keen to start your teaching placement: a good first impression. So what goes in this file?

You will use your school experience file day to day over the coming weeks of your practice. In the first instance you are advised to read the documentation for your school placement contained within any school experience handbook. More often than not, information about what should go in this file will be detailed in the appropriate handbook or guidance and will aid your preparation. Examples of the items that you might place in this file are:

*   school information sheet;

*   emergency contact details;

*   forms needed for the placement;

*   pre- and post-practice tutorial records;

*   information related to the roles of staff (when known);

*   teaching timetable (when known);

*   file dividers for each section (consult school experience handbooks for details), eg daily planning, assessment, policies, weekly review meetings, lesson evaluations.

Professional development profile or training file

Often referred to as the professional development profile or the PDP for short, this file will track your development against the Teachers' Standards (DfE, 2011c). It is advisable, before your first school experience, to set up a page for each Standard or sub-Standard. It is probable that you will be expected to write evaluative critical reflections related to your development against each part of the Standards. Furthermore you will need to collect and collate evidence that will support your claims of meeting the Standards. It is a good idea to think how you might organise this element. Your university or college may be happy for you to cross-reference evidence held in your school experience file while others want the evidence in the PDP. Check with the school experience documentation or your supervisory tutor as to how your files should be organised. Additionally, you do not need to wait until your school placement to use your PDP. Throughout your training programme and taught input at college you will be learning new knowledge that should spark your reflection. Why not record these in your PDP where they can contribute to the evidence base against the Standards?

A record of targets may also be placed in this file, and you will be expected to review the Standards with your supervisory tutor in order to set development targets for the placement: a pre-practice tutorial. Clearly on your inaugural placement, the entire Teachers' Standards are targets, so you may just have a briefing from your college or a group meeting rather than an individual tutorial to set targets.

Joining a teaching union

No matter what your political inclination is, it is highly advisable that you join a teaching union. At this point in your teaching career simply joining a union is more important than finding one that reflects your views. Belonging to a teaching union prior to entering a school context will help protect you from many eventualities. They each provide different insurance benefits, such as:

- cover of personal property;
- accident cover;
- legal services.

Many unions also offer additional benefits such as motor insurance, travel services and teaching resources such as planners, diaries, calendars and pens. More often than not, your provider will arrange an open day where you can meet a variety of union representatives. It is usually free for trainee teachers to join. A list of the main teaching unions is available in the Taking it further section of this chapter.

Educational jargon

Although you will have come across some educational jargon in the taught aspects of your course, it is likely that you will meet new educational jargon while on your initial visit and throughout your placement. If this is the case, keep a note in your placement file of all the terms you see, hear and read, as it will be valuable for future reference. Do not be afraid to ask the class teacher (when appropriate) to explain what they mean. Teaching is a profession that is full of three-letter acronyms. Even for experienced teachers new acronyms are always appearing. Educational jargon can in itself be a challenge to make sense of and get your head around. Unfortunately we do not have the room to provide an exhaustive list of acronyms that you might encounter but some of the more commonly used terms are listed in the glossary at the end of this book.

School expectations

Dress code

It is important that you dress appropriately throughout your time in school. Often there are unspoken rules about what to wear; however, if you use your common sense you will not go too far wrong. For your first visit, it is advisable to be dressed smartly but practically. You may have to go outside, for example for a PE lesson on the school field. In this instance stiletto heels may not be the most practical of foot attire! How you visually present to pupils, colleagues and parents can significantly influence the way in which you are perceived. It is a well-known fact that we judge and make decisions about a person's character in fewer than ten seconds, therefore, as a role model, try to ensure that you avoid outrageous hairstyles, revealing clothes and cover any visible piercings.

Staffroom etiquette

While the staffroom may offer you sanctuary from the pupils, it is imperative that you are mindful of those who frequent it. On the surface the staffroom will appear innocuous but it contains adults who are representative of the school's different stakeholders: parents, governors, advisors, outside agencies, etc.

Critical questions

»   *What are the possible implications of discussing pupil matters in the staffroom?*

»   *Where should you discuss pupils?*

»   *You have started to form an opinion about another member of staff. Where would you discuss this matter?*

Pupil issues should be discussed in the privacy of your own classroom with only you and your class teacher present. This will protect you from any claims related to breaches of confidentiality. Often teaching assistants are also parents of children in the school. Alternatively, teaching assistants will be friends with other parents outside of school. If you inadvertently discuss a pupil in the confines of the staffroom and in earshot of other adults, you run the risk of this information returning to the parent of the pupil concerned. Under no circumstance should you discuss another member of staff. If you have issues that relate to a member of staff then the guidance given later in this chapter will support you.

Confidentiality

In your role as a trainee teacher you will be party to confidential information relating to pupils and on occasions home backgrounds. You should ensure that you do not breach any confidentiality expectations. A good rule of thumb is to not divulge any information that you glean in school to anyone, not even a teaching assistant from another class.

School policies

Schools are awash with policies; however, it is your duty to make yourself familiar with them. There are some key policies that you should be aware of, for example:

- the behaviour policy;

- the marking policy;

- the safeguarding policy.

Critical questions

»   *Why are the three policies mentioned above key to your placement?*

»   *What other policies do you think are important for you to read and why?*

»   *How do you believe the policies will impact on your placement?*

The behaviour policy (which is covered in more depth in Chapter 5 of this book) seeks to support you in your behaviour management by outlining the whole school approach taken to discipline. It provides you with clear guidance on rewards and sanctions enforced in the school and charts the whole school rules that you should be conversant with. The marking policy shapes any marking that you undertake. All written feedback should be in accordance with its instructions. There may be a mark scheme that is used across the school and you should ensure that you follow this for consistency. Finally a school's safeguarding policy and procedure document is an essential read to ensure that you are fully acquainted with it in the event that a child discloses a safeguarding issue to you. Remember you, and everyone who comes into contact with pupils and their families, has an important role to play in safeguarding children (DfE, 2014a).

CASE STUDY

Jonah's safeguarding story

My placement was going really well and I was thoroughly enjoying working with the children. Things changed, however, on my fourth week when I met a tearful lad in the corridor one morning. I had already established a good relationship with the boy and he seemed to look up to me as a role model. He was rather quiet and I'd been told that his mother was, well ... a little unusual. I asked him what the matter was and he just looked at me and then lifted his jumper and shirt up. Oh my word! I was just so shocked! All I could see was this huge carpet burn that covered the whole of his back. I went into panic and started asking lots of questions. I remembered that we'd had some input about safeguarding at college but it was right at the start of the course and I couldn't remember a thing and the school hadn't given me any information. I just didn't know what to do in this situation.

Critical questions

»   *When starting your placement, whose responsibility is it to find out about the safeguarding procedures?*

» *If you were unsure about the procedures, when would you deal with this? Who would you go to?*

» *Was Jonah right to ask lots of questions?*

» *If presented with a safeguarding issue on placement, would you know who to speak to?*

» *Consider your placement and draw a flowchart of the safeguarding process you would go through and the people you would speak to.*

» *What other key information do you need to remember? Write the key information up and keep it as a checklist for your placement.*

If a child reveals that they might be at risk then you should follow local safeguarding procedures immediately. Make yourself familiar with these from the start of the placement! You should, for example, know the name of the lead professional responsible for safeguarding within the school. Prior to any placement review your understanding of what to do if a child discloses, you witness something unusual or a change in a pupil's behaviour. Most importantly do not tell the child that you will keep a secret. There is a duty placed on you to pass on any information related to safeguarding to the designated safeguarding individual. You must, however, ensure confidentiality with those outside the parameters of the permitted safeguarding procedures for sharing information. Should you want more support on this topic a good source of advice is available at the NSPCC website http://www.nspcc.org.uk/preventing-abuse/keeping-children-safe/

It is prudent to make yourself aware of any child protection concerns surrounding the taking of photos while on your placement, and also internet safety. As part of your teacher training course you might be expected or choose to use photographs as evidence for your PDP. It is imperative that you find out what the protocol is prior to capturing any image. Likewise, are you familiar with internet safety? You may have received Child Exploitation Online Protection (CEOP) training in this area but, if not, the CEOP 'Thinkuknow' website (http://www.thinkuknow.co.uk) provides some helpful information.

Extended thinking

» *Whose responsibility is it to safeguard the well-being of pupils?*

» *What are the key aspects when keeping children safe?*

Time management

Arriving and departing school

Make sure you know what time school starts and more importantly the expected time of your arrival. Arriving in advance of the expected time indicates your professional enthusiasm for teaching and keenness to be well prepared for the day ahead. Even if you are not teaching that morning, arriving early and showing willing by volunteering to assist your mentor or class teacher in their preparation for the day is always very welcome. So what if you are continually late at the beginning of the day? Consider the case studies below. Carole is the mentor, Helen the trainee teacher and Jim the supervisory tutor.

CASE STUDY

Carole's story

Helen was well-mannered and arrived punctually for the first week and then things started to deteriorate. I tackled Helen about her scraping through the door at 8:30, the appointed time to arrive, I grant, but with no time spare for us to catch up before the day began. The following week, the majority of days were fine but then it became even worse. On some days Helen managed to arrive at 8:30 but more often than not it was nearer 9am. Helen had even taken to planning her lessons while I was teaching. She never had resources ready and was very ill-prepared. I asked if anything was wrong or if she needed any further support from me. Helen said she was fine, that she felt well-supported and that she would try to arrive in a more timely manner in future. Things didn't improve and I had to call in Jim, her supervisory tutor.

Critical questions

» What impact does Helen's late arrival have on her teaching?

» What impact does Helen's late arrival have on a) Carole's day and b) the pupils' day?

» How might Helen's late arrival ultimately impact on her placement?

» List the Teachers' Standards Helen is failing to meet.

CASE STUDY

Jim's story

Well, I got a call from Carole who explained the situation with Helen over the phone. It did indeed sound as though there were serious issues so I arranged to call in at the school the next day. I arrived before Helen, which just served to highlight the concerns that Carole had. I asked Helen how she thought the placement was progressing and she was really happy with where she had been placed and thought she was doing really well. I quizzed her then about the time-keeping, asking how she thought Carole might view things. At first Helen said that she arrived at 8:30am every day, and as this was the appointed time she couldn't see that this was an issue, so Carole should not have an issue with that. I agreed that on occasions this wouldn't be too much of a concern, however I went on to enquire about the consistency of the lateness and the ever-increasing move towards 9am rather than 8:30am. I asked her if she had considered how the pupils might be affected. At this point Helen just cried, and through her sobbing she started to open up.

Critical questions

» Recall the information you read in Chapter 1. How reflective is Helen?

» What model of reflection is Jim trying to get Helen to use?

» How does Jim's level of questioning support Helen's reflections?

CASE STUDY

Helen's story

I was really excited about starting my placement and looking forward to working with the class. Carole was very supportive and I wanted to do my best. The first week went well but then things became more difficult as the amount of preparation and teaching increased. I was having difficulties with my car and had recently been thrown out of home. I had no money to get the car fixed and was having to work after I finished school so that I could afford to eat. I wasn't finished at work until midnight and then all I was physically and mentally capable of was sleep. I wanted to tell Carole but didn't know what she'd think of me and I was conscious that I needed to remain professional; sharing my personal problems with Carole didn't seem right somehow. When Jim arrived and questioned me, I had to be honest with myself. I knew I wasn't coping and Jim made me realise the significance and impact my personal problems were having on Carole and the pupils in the class.

Critical questions

» *What do you consider to be the professional issues in this case?*

» *Is there anything that Helen or Carole could have done differently?*

» *Does Carole have a duty of care to Helen?*

There are often multiple perspectives surrounding a concern, but if you think your personal situation might harm your placement, you are strongly advised to seek advice from your supervisory tutor. Your tutor is there to support you and will make a professional judgement as to whether the information needs to be shared with your mentor.

Likewise the same is true when you are considering leaving school at the end of the day. As a teacher you have contracted contact hours to fulfil and these extend beyond those timetabled. Confirm with your mentor the time at which you can leave and then work past this in order to complete the planning or preparation of resources for the next day. There is nothing better than going home after an exhausting day knowing that when you walk in to school the next morning everything is neatly laid out at the front of the class in readiness for your teaching!

Managing your time throughout the school day is equally as important. You will obviously want to fit into the school team but take care that you do not loiter in the staffroom. You will be expected to collect children from the playground after their break times or assemblies. In the role of 'loco parentis' while children are in school you are responsible not only for their education but their health, well-being and safety. Unsupervised children can (on occasions) result in accidents. Imagine for example if you are late back to your classroom and the children have been left unattended.

Critical questions

» *List any misfortunes that potentially could arise if children are left unsupervised in class or outside.*

» *What impact might these have on you as a trainee teacher?*

» *How can you ensure that children are supervised if you are detained for any reason?*

Additional placement duties

There will almost certainly be an expectation that you will attend whole school assemblies and contribute to other aspects of wider school life. While it is tempting to see these and other times such as playground duty as a chance to work on planning or the preparation of resources, you must remember that you are now working as a teacher. You should also consider how you might assist with extra-curricular activities. Currently you may not feel confident enough to volunteer to run an extra-curricular club but have you asked your mentor if you can help with the sewing club or with football practice?

ITE provider expectations

You will have certain expectations placed upon you by your training provider which you will be required to undertake prior to, during and after your school experience. For example, you may be required to complete additional school-based tasks. These will need scheduling with the help of the mentor so that you complete any assessments before the end of the placement. Below are a few of the expectations you might encounter:

- a pre-practice tutorial;
- school-based tasks;
- use of an email address that is professional in nature rather than personal (eg pinkfairy@hotmail.com);
- files to remain with you in placement at all times;
- weekly review meetings with your mentor;
- lesson evaluations;
- lesson observations of you and others;
- a post-practice tutorial.

Consult your college's documentation to ascertain what additional expectations you have to meet in order to pass the placement.

You may also discover that you have a paired placement rather than an individual placement. Do not worry about this as it will afford you a diverse experience. A paired placement presents many more opportunities to team-plan and teach with your peer. Bouncing ideas off each other and playing to one another's strengths will enhance your practice.

Wider expectations

You are strongly recommended to read the Bristol Guide (University of Bristol, 2008), which outlines the roles and responsibilities placed upon you as a teacher. While not a scintillating read, it clearly outlines and explains the statutory legal framework within which you will be working.

Extended thinking

»   *What are the top ten items needed for a successful practice?*

»   *How would you rank them in priority?*

Chapter reflections

Many of the practical details related to your school placement are common sense, but that also makes them quite easy to overlook. While most are small things, they can make a big difference to your overall experience and the way in which you are perceived. Perhaps make yourself a list of the key ideas in this chapter so that you can remember them more easily and refer to them before your placement and at the beginning of each school day.

Critical points

»   *You only get one chance to make a first impression – make sure it is the best one!*

»   *Show willing.*

»   *Assume the characteristics of a teacher from the beginning.*

»   *Exhibit your duty of care to your pupils and others in the school.*

»   *Seek professional help, guidance and support as necessary.*

Taking it further

Association of Teachers and Lecturers (ATL). www.atl.org.uk/.

Children's Workforce Development Council (CWDC) (2009) *Early Identification, Assessment of Needs and Intervention: The Common Assessment Framework for Children and Young People: A Guide for Practitioners.* www.education.gov.uk/publications/eOrderingDownload/CAF-Practitioner-Guide.pdf. Accessed 5 March 2013.

DfES (2007) *Statutory Guidance on Making Arrangements to Safeguard and Promote the Welfare of Children under Section 11 of the Children Act 2004.* www.education.gov.uk/publications/standard/publicationDetail/Page1/DFES-0036-2007. Accessed 5 March 2013.

National Association of School Masters/Union of Women Teachers (NASUWT). www.nasuwt.org.uk/index.htm.

National Union of Teachers (NUT). www.teachers.org.uk/.

4 Collaborative professional partnerships

Setting up or getting involved in a curriculum information meeting

Home–school diaries

Working with parents and carers

Attending parents' evenings

Getting involved with the PA/PTA

Working with outside agencies

Collaborative professional partnerships

Working with teaching assistants and other adults in the classroom

The mentor relationship

Mentoring and coaching in Initial Teacher Education

The changing nature of the relationship

Defining mentoring and coaching

Mentor attributes and competencies

Teachers' Standards (DfE, 2011c)

8 Fulfil wider professional responsibilities

- make a positive contribution to the wider life and ethos of the school

- develop effective professional relationships with colleagues, knowing how and when to draw on advice and specialist support

- deploy support staff effectively

- take responsibility for improving teaching through appropriate professional development, responding to advice and feedback from colleagues

- communicate effectively with parents with regard to pupils' achievements and well-being.

Introduction

It is essential for you to understand that you cannot work in isolation while on placement. Primarily you should draw upon and utilise all the human resources, expertise and experience offered to you. At the heart of every successful placement are the relationships you cultivate with the whole of your placement community. It is not enough solely to work on forming positive and professional relationships with the pupils. You need to view the entire school community as 'collaborative partners', each of whom will have a part to play in the success or otherwise of your teaching placement. Your partners will range from the caretaker to the lunchtime supervisor, from parents to teaching assistants, as well as the senior management team, teaching staff and outside agencies. So how could all these individuals possibly have an impact on the success of your placement?

This chapter sets out the key people you may encounter and how they may impact on your placement. You are given the opportunity to evaluate a range of case studies in order to understand the intricacies you will encounter when working with a diverse group of people in a school setting. These will support your preparation for your school placement and into your future teaching career.

Working with parents and carers

It is important that you establish effective home–school links in order to support pupils. Some schools encourage parental and carer involvement, both through organisations such as the PTA (Parent Teacher Association) and as volunteers in the classroom; others prefer the parents to remain outside the school gates and to interact with the teaching staff only as part of the reporting process at scheduled parents' evenings. Do check with your mentor if the school has a policy detailing the expectations and accepted practices when dealing with parents/and carers.

CASE STUDY

Becki's parent dilemma

I really believe that getting to know the parents can help me understand the pupils better, so at the end of my first day in placement, I opened the classroom door into the playground and stepped outside with the children, nodding and smiling at the parents. A parent rushed over and, standing really close to me, started to demand information about her son's achievement that day. She was actually quite intimidating! I found myself backing away towards the door, trying to remember what we had done and how her son had performed. My mentor stepped in the moment she realised what was happening and politely directed me inside 'for a meeting', and afterwards she told me it was a school policy that parents are instructed to see the office to make an appointment if they wish to speak to teachers and that all appointments go through the head teacher first. This was because in the past there had been incidents where parents had become threatening towards teachers and the head felt it was the best way to prevent this happening again. But I still feel I need to speak to the parents if I am truly going to support the pupils, and I am uncomfortable with ignoring them or sending them away when they are just concerned about their children. How can I do this without going against school policy?

Critical questions

» What advice would you give Becki in addressing this situation?

» From whom could she seek advice?

» What do you think are the key reasons for effective communication between parents and teachers? List at least five, and think about how each affects the regularity of communication.

Regardless of the ethos of the school, it is a requirement of the Teachers' Standards (DfE, 2012f) that you demonstrate effective communication with parents regarding pupils' progress and pastoral issues. Such involvement of parents in a child's education has multiple benefits which have been shown (Bastiani, 2003) to include improvements in behaviour and attainment. Given the prominence in the new Special Needs and Disability Code of Practice (DfE, 2014b) where the views, wishes and feelings of a young person, and their parents are paramount this is an aspect of practice which is vital to excel at. So how can this be achieved? Your school environment may have a range of approaches, but here is a selection of strategies which can be implemented as part of a placement if needed, with the agreement of your mentor, to enable you to meet the Standards.

Home–school diaries

EYFS and Key Stage 1 settings often have, at the very least, a reading diary in which parents are encouraged to write alongside comments from teachers and TAs. This can be used to pass information to parents and to seek answers to questions regarding pupils' circumstances, but it would be worth considering the benefit of having a separate home–school communication book to distinguish it from a particular curriculum area. Often such diaries are only given to those with particular needs or issues, which can, however, lead to pupils and parents feeling victimised or insulted.

CASE STUDY

A parent's story

My son started at the local school nursery after two years in a private day nursery as I wanted him to get to know the children he would be starting school with. I work full time, so he is dropped off by his dad and his granddad on different days, but I joined the PTA and attended the Christmas fayre as a volunteer to show I wanted to be involved. Then last Friday the teacher sent home a 'Behaviour Diary', with a note to say that because they 'never see Mummy' they felt this would be a good way of communicating issues. I was appalled! Not only did sending it on a Friday mean I couldn't speak to anyone or ask questions, additionally the teacher has never tried to phone me or speak to my husband about any issues. It has made me question whether I want my son at the school at all!

Critical questions

»   *Communicating with parents requires sensitivity. How could the behaviour diary above have been shared with the parent in order to establish an effective partnership?*

»   *Try writing the covering letter that could have been sent home with the diary.*

Getting involved with the PA/PTA

Most schools have a parents' association (PA), PTA or a friends' association (for definitions of the different types of association see http://pta.org.uk/pta-info-centre/pta-info-sheets/running-your-pta/starting-a-pta/). Whatever form this takes in your school setting it is worth considering attending a meeting if possible (the school diary should have a record of the dates for you to see if any are being held during your placement) or making contact with the association through members of the committee in order to find out what activities and events they are planning over the term.

PTA-UK is a registered charity: the majority of school associations see fundraising as a key aspect of their role, but there is a range of ways that schools and their parent bodies work in order to enhance learning, so do investigate how it works in your setting.

Attending parents' evenings

You may have the opportunity during placement to shadow your mentor at a parents' evening. It is strongly advisable that you take advantage of such a chance, as learning appropriate ways of speaking to parents about their children will enable you to be more effective in your own practice. Even though you are not conducting the parents' evening yourself remember you are representing the school, so remain as professional and as presentable as possible: any parent you speak to will be forming opinions about their child's experience and making judgements about the quality of education being provided.

It is important that you remember that it is the class teacher's responsibility to provide the parents with a progress report, so unless you are invited to comment it is advisable to just listen carefully to how the teacher interacts with parents and carers. What you perceive to be a helpful comment about a child's behaviour, for example, could be misinterpreted or be contrary to previous discussions that the teacher and parents have had. In addition, it is vital you remember that other children should not be discussed or referred to, even if they are mentioned by the parents in relation to their own child.

Setting up or getting involved in a curriculum information meeting

If there are no scheduled parents' evenings during your placement there are other ways of meeting your pupils' families. Some schools have regular after-school presentation evenings for parents and carers in order to discuss curriculum changes and the intended learning for the coming half term or to inform the parents of a particular issue such as internet safety. With the support of your mentor you could think about taking part in (or even organising!) an event one evening to inform parents of the topics you intend to cover or a current curriculum area such as the teaching of synthetic phonics.

Critical question

» *Families are diverse: some children may not live with both parents, others may have same-sex parents or live with foster carers, etc. When communicating through letters or in other ways, how can you ensure you are being inclusive of different family compositions?*

Extended thinking

» *Who are the key stakeholders in a child's education?*

» *What contribution can you make to the ethos of a school?*

Working with teaching assistants and other adults in the classroom

As a class teacher it is your responsibility to plan for and manage the learning for your class, including the use of support staff. Many other adults are involved in supporting pupils and teachers in school, and it is important you are clear on the roles and responsibilities for each one. Administrative staff are often able to provide copies of policy documents and general school information; school caretakers can be informative regarding facilities; lunchtime supervisors can be helpful in identifying pupil behaviour issues in free time that might affect subsequent lessons. It is important to consider how an effective relationship with each of these colleagues might be formed and to ensure you are proactive in establishing these.

In addition to your mentor teacher the most frequently observed professional relationship will be with teaching assistants, or TAs. TAs are an integral part of primary school practice, particularly in the Early Years, and it is important you understand how to plan appropriately for any other adults involved in the children's learning. Research such as Blanchford et al. (2009) clearly indicate how pupils' needs are routinely met by TAs and the vital role they now play in planning and supporting pupils by intervention programmes. The deployment of TAs can be done in a number of ways depending on the specific role of the TA within the school.

Ascertaining their role is a good place to start: is your TA a classroom teaching assistant or a learning support assistant, for example? This might inform you of what they expect from their role.

CASE STUDY

Andy and the TA's story (part 1)

During my final teaching practice I was really excited about teaching my Year 3 class, which included a child with autism. He had Mrs Khan to support him, and in my first meeting with her she made it clear she was there for him and not me in lessons. Before my first whole class teaching session I gave her a copy of my plan, which she put down in the staffroom and left there. In the lesson (numeracy) I was aware of Mrs Khan talking to the pupil throughout my starter activity, which I found really distracting. I raised it with the class teacher, who said she understood as she found the TA did the same in her lessons and that I would get used to it.

Critical questions

» What are the key issues in the scenario above? Consider the implications for: a) Andy (the student teacher), b) the pupil, c) Mrs Khan (the TA), d) the class teacher.

» Who else might need to be involved in addressing the issues?

» List three strategies you could use to address each issue in order to improve the relationship with Mrs Khan.

There is very rarely only one side to any professional relationship, and it is always worth considering the possible reasons for a colleague's action. Consider how the TA in Andy's scenario might actually be feeling.

CASE STUDY

Andy and the TA's story (part 2)

I've been a general TA for a number of years now, but last year when a child with autism joined the school I successfully applied to work with him one-to-one. However, some members of staff don't seem to realise my hours are all linked to supporting him now: I get asked to do photocopying, sort out noticeboards, etc. and I've had to be quite forceful in reminding them that I have a new role. Whenever we have a new person in the class I have to work especially hard making sure that the pupil concerned stays calm as he doesn't respond well to change: sometimes just a quiet dialogue in his ear, reminding him it's okay and what the new person is there to do is enough.

Critical questions

» Does this knowledge change your view of the key issues for the student teacher? Why?

» Reflect on your list of strategies to address the issues: would you add/adapt anything in light of the alternative viewpoint?

While it is preferable to work collaboratively with a TA it is important you consider the requirement for you to demonstrate that you can *deploy support staff effectively* (DfE, 2012f). When you are in the role of class teacher it is your responsibility to plan for the learning, and this includes allocating specific roles or tasks for support staff. Working collaboratively should not mean that the TA is expected to plan a small group activity, unless they are a higher level teaching assistant (HLTA), while you concentrate on planning for the rest of the class. TAs often know the children very well, both pastorally and academically, and can inform your planning by sharing their insights, but it is up to you to plan the way their support will be managed in the classroom.

There are several models for deploying staff as part of your classroom practice. The most frequently used are as follows.

1) **Room management** allows you as the trainee to establish how you wish to organise support staff and match them to groups of pupils when a TA has not been assigned to a particular pupil. It assumes that roles and responsibilities within the classroom have been allocated based on the lesson, the needs of the pupils and the intended activity.

2) **Zoning** is a more flexible approach, often observed in classrooms where teacher and TA have worked together effectively for a period of time: staff members support the pupils within particular 'zones' in the classroom rather than work with identified groups or individuals.

3) **Reflective teamwork** extends and builds upon the 'room management' approach, where staff members discuss not only the pupils' learning in detail but also how they will work together to progress the learning.

(Cremin, Thomas and Vincett, 2005, page 416)

Critical questions

» Conduct a series of focused observations where you try to identify how the TA is being deployed. Which of the above models are reflected in these scenarios?

» Identify possible strategies for deploying support staff by completing the table below:

Five key ways a TA could support pupils	Five key ways a TA could support the teacher
1	1
2	2
3	3
4	4
5	5

Extended thinking

» Rate yourself from 1 to 5, 1 being most successful and 5 least successful, on how you feel able to deploy a TA in a classroom.

» What improvements in your practice might be needed to raise your grading?

Working with outside agencies

When you begin a teaching practice placement you become a staff member of the school, and much of your non-contact time will be spent learning to work effectively with your colleagues. However, there is often a lot of inter-agency work happening within the school environment and it is worth making yourself familiar with the different specialist organisations or individuals you may come across. This will enable you, if necessary, to *draw on advice and specialist support* (DfE, 2012f) beyond the expertise found in school.

Within the school it is the role of the Special Educational Needs Co-ordinator (SENCO) and Child Protection Officer (CPO) to ensure that any specific additional needs of the children are being met, so it is worth asking to speak to them (if they are not your mentor teacher). You can ask general questions about the school's policy for dealing with issues of child protection, for example, or more specific questions relating to members of your class. It is important to remember that some of the information may be highly confidential and/or sensitive, so if it is necessary to make notes ensure that these are kept securely filed for your reference only.

The SENCO and CPO will be able to tell you what other agencies are currently working within the school, either through a local authority service level agreement or individual arrangement. These can include the school nurse, the educational welfare officer, speech and language therapists or social services, to name but a few. If pupils in your class are receiving support it is vital you familiarise yourself with the issues as well as the role played by the specialist: this will enable you to know what advice they may be able to offer. It is highly unlikely you will need to deal with these other agencies as a trainee, although you may be invited to shadow your mentor in meetings to discuss individual children in your class. In this case the same issues of confidentiality and sensitivity highlighted above would be relevant.

Mentoring and coaching in Initial Teacher Education

Whether you are studying for a three- or four-year Initial Teacher Education (ITE) undergraduate degree, undertaking a PGCE or following an employment-based route such as School Direct, School Direct (Salaried), GTP or Assessment Only, you will be assigned a mentor. You should not underestimate the importance of the role of your mentor. It is undisputed that your mentor will be instrumental in assisting you in developing your competencies as a teacher. This assertion is echoed, for example, by Griffiths (2007, page 120) who highlighted that trainee teachers especially valued *the personal support ... they received from their mentor and other staff, as this had a direct effect on their self-confidence and perceived ability to make progress.*

Defining mentoring and coaching

So what is your view of mentoring and coaching in ITE? Have a look at the tasks and questions below and try to define mentoring and coaching.

Critical questions

» *Write a definition for mentoring.*

» *Write a definition for coaching.*

»   *How do the definitions differ?*

»   *What are your expectations?*

»   *Would you prefer to have a mentor on placement or a coach? Why?*

»   *How do you think your view might change over the course of your initial teacher training?*

Do not worry if at this point you are unsure as to the difference between a mentor and a coach. By the end of this chapter you should be able to identify the subtle differences between the two and appreciate how the relationship between you and your mentor will change over time. This change in relationship will be identifiable not just within the course of your first school experience but throughout your training as you gain confidence and experience in conjunction with enhanced levels of reflection.

Definitions for mentoring and coaching are often open to a range of interpretations, hence you may have struggled defining the two. Many writers regard mentoring as an individual consciousness, integrated in a long-term perceptive activity. The CUREE (2005) document, however, defines mentoring as developing short-term skills grounded in induction. Briefly, a mentor takes a 'directive' approach to your development by explicitly stating what you need to do, when you need to do it and how. A coach generally takes a 'non-directive' approach, encouraging you to take responsibility for your own development through the art of coaching conversations. You are encouraged to draw on your level of reflection and experience in order to evaluate your learning, identify personal targets and ways of achieving these. For our purposes the term 'mentoring' will be used throughout, although your mentor may well be acting in coach mode at certain periods on your placement. In your placement context, your mentor is someone who is involved with you in a developmental and supportive relationship. They have the potential influence to affect your growth and learning both personally and professionally.

Take a look at the next two case studies and see if you can identify when the mentor is in 'mentor' mode or 'coach' mode.

CASE STUDIES

Sue's lesson observation feedback

Mentor: *Well, that was an interesting lesson. What was it that you wanted the children to learn?*

Sue: *I wanted to get the children to plan a fair test to find out where the seeds would germinate the best. They needed to identify the variables and recognise that only one could change.*

Mentor: *What did you feel pleased with?*

Sue: *Ah, well! I thought they worked well in their groups and planned carefully. Most groups I felt had understood that they only needed to change one variable, however when I started to check I could see that some still had changed more than one so we had a discussion about this. I used this as an opportunity to stop the children and conduct a mini-plenary. This worked well as the children were* able to voice their plans and the children became involved in peer assessment. I was really pleased with that aspect of the lesson.

Mentor: How did the lesson extend the children's understanding?

Sue: OK, our previous lesson had focused on parts of a plant and the conditions children thought they needed to grow. They had hypothesised but I wanted to get them to test out their hypotheses. More importantly though was to check to see if they could plan a fair test and this was where some children still had problems.

Mentor: How does this relate to your development as a teacher?

Sue: Wow, um, it relates to certain areas I've been working on recently, actually. I have been focusing on my questioning skills and giving feedback as part of the assessment process. I made a purposeful effort to get around the children in order to ask questions, which in turn led to me discovering that some pupils were having issues. When we previously chatted I asked about the notion of using mini-plenaries as a way of dispelling misconceptions and I set this as one of my targets. I felt that the mini-plenary helped to address the misconceptions really well as the children were able to re-focus and achieve the objective.

Mentor: Anything else?

Sue: I've also been working on getting the children to peer-review. So today when they were asked to feed back to each other in groups about their fair tests, it helped them to identify any errors they had in their own plans. I think I'd like to try this more often and include self-assessment too.

Mentor: So how do you think you might achieve that?

Sue: Well it might be a bit difficult as I don't think they've done much self-assessment so far, certainly not with me. I think I'd need to model it perhaps in the first instance. I've also seen the class teacher using some Assessment for Learning (AfL) strategies (AfL is addressed in Chapter 6) and perhaps I should include these in my teaching next time. What do you think?

Sundeep's lesson observation feedback

Mentor: Well done, Sundeep! That art lesson went quite well. The children were engaged and produced some reasonable work. They seemed to like the activity you set for them.

Sundeep: Yes, I was pleased with the pictures they made too. I could see they were having fun, which is what I wanted.

Mentor: I did think, however, that you could have modelled the technique of how to achieve perspective. Some of the children were unsure as to how to do this and the pictures illustrate this. You should have intervened sooner when you realised that they were hesitant to put pencil to paper.

Sundeep: I hadn't really thought about that to be truthful. I talked about perspective and thought that would be enough. I didn't notice that the children were struggling. What should I have done?

Mentor: Well, firstly you could have used a large sheet of paper and discussed how to draw in the lines of perspective to draw the eye into the picture. Simultaneously you should have drawn these lines so that the children had a clear example. If you had done this, the children would have achieved a better outcome.

Sundeep: Ok. I'll remember that.

Mentor: Then you should have checked with the children to see if they knew what was expected of them before they started the task and asked how they were going to achieve it. You could have brought someone to the front of the class to demonstrate. This would have given you some feedback on what the children knew about the task before they set about it. You then should have circulated around the class more. Moving in and out of the children and questioning them would have informed you about how the class as a whole were feeling about the activity. You can try this next week when you teach art again. That can be one of your targets this week.

Sundeep: Alright, that sounds sensible but I must admit that art isn't my strongest subject. I'm not sure that any amount of modelling or checking will make much difference. I thought that the work they did was all right and they were having fun! Art should be about relaxation, can't they just draw?

Critical questions

» Which mentor is using a mentoring approach and which is using a coaching approach?

» What evidence do you have?

» List how the coaching approach promotes trainee reflection.

» Which approach would you prefer? Why?

» When do you think each approach would be used?

» What key facets are important as a trainee when receiving lesson feedback?

Mentor attributes and competencies

The importance of the mentor's role is undisputed; however, the role of your mentor may vary throughout your placement. No matter what stage of a school placement you find yourself in, mentors need to demonstrate that they have certain attributes and are competent in the mentoring process. Consider the attributes and competencies you believe a professional mentor should possess.

Critical questions

» What attributes or competencies would you expect to identify in your mentor?

» How might an attribute or competency be exhibited in your mentor's practice?

» List the attributes and competencies in the table below, stating how the attribute or competency might be displayed in reality.

Attribute/competency	How might this attribute/competency manifest itself to you while on a school placement?

The following are examples of professional mentors' attributes and competencies. This is not an exhaustive list by any means and you are directed to the likes of Clutterbuck (2000) for supplementary guidance. Literature such as Gravells and Wallace (2012) will also help you start to understand the complex practical, moral and behavioural issues linked to the mentoring relationship.

Mentor competencies embrace those of:

- **facilitator** – they provide opportunities for you to conduct observations of others, and suggest key people to talk to, eg the mathematics co-ordinator;

- **supervisor** – they make it their business to find out from others how you are performing in order to deal with any difficulties that might arise;

- **assessor** – they observe your practice and make assessment judgements against the Teachers' Standards (DfE, 2012f);

- **reviewer** – they review your progress weekly against the Teachers' Standards and reflect upon your ability to act upon advice given through the mentoring and coaching process;

- **setter of targets** – based upon their assessments and weekly review meetings they set targets against the standards for you to work towards;

- **critical friend** – they give developmental feedback after each lesson observation. This may be achieved through a directive model, eg telling you what went well or not so well, or a more non-directive coaching model, eg asking questions, using the GROW model (Whitmore, 2002).

Attributes of individual mentors might comprise:

- approachable;

- empathic;

- good listener;

- honest;

- supportive.

Bear in mind, however, that not all professional mentors will necessarily exhibit all the above competencies or attributes. What is important is that you draw on the professional mentor's knowledge and capabilities in order to develop your practice as effectively as possible.

The mentor relationship

The effectiveness of the mentoring relationship is dependent on what you see as being the role of the professional mentor or coach while you are on your school placement. What are your expectations from your mentor relationship? What do you want to get from the relationship? If you actively seek out specialist professional expertise from your mentor and respond positively, you will acquire and adapt to new knowledge more readily. This will result in a co-coaching relationship whereby you are seen as a co-worker and given support accordingly. If you are less reflective and less proactive you will find that you will have to react and respond to more directive hierarchical support from your mentor. Which would you like to aim for?

Mentors are sometimes your assessor as well as your mentor. You may therefore find that you are assigned a mentor and a class teacher to work with. This enables the mentor to retain a professional, almost detached working relationship with you, allowing the class teacher to assist you with planning and give you informal daily feedback. Your mentor will invariably conduct a weekly meeting with you to review progress and set targets for the forthcoming week. They may conduct joint observations of your teaching with either the class teacher or another member of the senior leadership team. You should not be alarmed by this. Your university or college tutor will also want to observe you teaching a lesson in conjunction with your mentor. This practice is conducted in order to moderate the judgements of mentors against the Teachers' Standards (DfE, 2012f).

The changing nature of the relationship

As you progress, so should your mentor's approach change towards you. This will stem from two pivotal characteristics:

1.   an established trusting and open professional relationship;

2.   escalation of your teaching experience along with deepened reflective dexterity.

You should find that there is a transition from a directive approach of mentor to one that is less directive and more a co-coach (CUREE, 2005). Your professional development is a journey and your mentor will move along a continuum between a mentor and coach depending on your role in the learning relationship.

Extended thinking

» *On a scale of 1 to 10 how would you rate your ability to accept constructive criticism?*

» *What would be the best bit of advice you could offer yourself when working with others in order to secure an improvement in your practice?*

Chapter reflections

Collaborative working in your placement setting with other adults and groups will assist you in meeting the Teachers' Standards (DfE, 2012f) effectively. It will also prepare you well for your future life as a teaching professional. By conducting yourself in a professional manner with all adults that you encounter on your school placement, you position yourself well to succeed. Establishing positive relationships with parents, carers and colleagues will ensure you are providing maximum benefit to the children you teach and will make your role both more wide-ranging and enjoyable. Your relationship with your mentor is an important part of your professional development, helping you develop key skills and enabling you to make the most of the learning opportunities during placement. As you become more reflective and experienced, your learning relationship with your professional mentor will develop.

Critical points

» *Always conduct yourself professionally with all stakeholders involved in the education of pupils at the school.*

» *Be proactive in developing relationships with parents, carers, colleagues and other adults.*

» *These relationships should be conducted within the constraints of any school protocols and policies.*

» *Make the most of the key professional learning relationship with your mentor.*

Taking it further

Blatchford, P, Bassett, P, Brown, P, and Martin, C (2009) Deployment and Impact of Support Staff Project. Available at https://www.uvm.edu/~cdci/evolveplus/documents/DCSF-RB148.pdf. (Accessed 5 March 2015.)

Edwards, A and Collison, J (1996) *Mentoring and Developing Practice in Primary Schools*. Buckingham: Open University Press.

Hobson, A (2002) Student Teachers' Perceptions of School-based Mentoring in Initial Teacher Training (ITT). *Mentoring and Tutoring: Partnership in Learning*, 10 (1): 5–20.

Morton, A (2003) *Mentoring*. York: LTSN.

Passmore, J (ed.) (2010) (2nd edn) *Excellence in Coaching: The Industry Guide*. London: Kogan Page.

Scanlon, L (2008) The Impact of Experience on Student Mentors' Conceptualisation of Mentoring. *International Journal of Evidence Based Coaching and Mentoring*, 6 (2): 57–66.

5 Behaviour management and classroom discipline

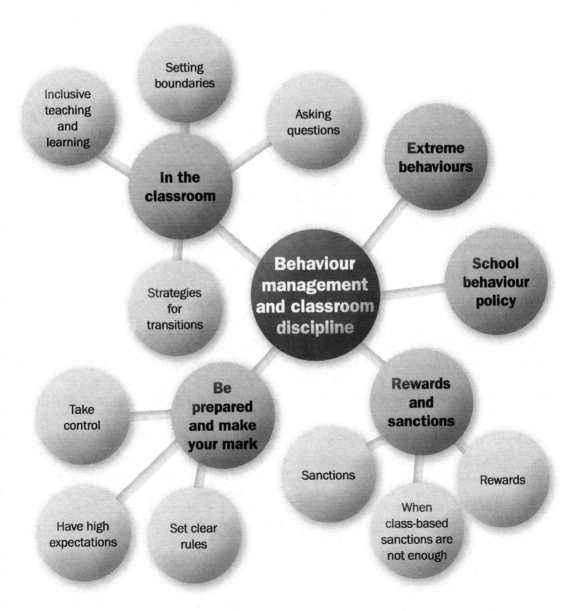

Teachers' Standards (DfE, 2011c)

7 Manage behaviour effectively to ensure a good and safe learning environment

- have clear rules and routines for behaviour in classrooms, and take responsibility for promoting good and courteous behaviour both in classrooms and around the school, in accordance with the school's behaviour policy

- have high expectations of behaviour, and establish a framework for discipline with a range of strategies, using praise, sanctions and rewards consistently and fairly

- manage classes effectively, using approaches which are appropriate to pupils' needs in order to involve and motivate them

- maintain good relationships with pupils, exercise appropriate authority and act decisively when necessary.

Introduction

Discipline in the classroom may be seen as the order that is vital so that teaching and learning may flourish, and it is because of this that it is important that all classrooms have discipline. As a new teacher it is fundamental to your practice that you realise that discipline and general teaching are one and the same and that they are not two separate items. It is important that you learn to accept that good teaching will lead to good discipline and you can foster this by your integrated use of behaviour management. As Steer (2009) rightly suggests, poor behaviours cannot be tolerated within any school setting since all children have the right to learn free from disruption. Given this, alongside a governmental backdrop of the need to raise standards, how teachers manage behaviour will always be under scrutiny both at local and national levels. For the most part, the behaviour that you will encounter in the classroom on a daily basis will be deemed low- and medium-level disruption. This will, for example, involve children wandering around, not paying attention, perhaps shouting out, talking and distracting others and other general work avoidance strategies such as having to over-sharpen a pencil. Most of these behaviours may be dealt with quite effectively under the general term behaviour for learning. This effectively means making work clear and easy to access, motivating and helping pupils should they have any problems. High-level disruption you will find is comparatively rare and may involve, for example, swearing, violence and theft. When these behaviours are encountered you will find they provide a challenge for the most experienced of staff and will no doubt involve severe punishments or sanctions, for example exclusion (not being allowed to attend school for a length of time).

Whatever behaviours you encounter, one of the key elements of managing classroom behaviour is the fostering of positive relationships with children. Given that each school is accountable for the quality of behaviour within their setting, not only to their stakeholders, but also to external bodies such as Ofsted (2012a) who are required to report upon the quality of behaviour within the school and while off site, it is of fundamental importance that this aspect of the Teachers' Standards is addressed successfully by all trainee teachers. It is understandable that for many of you new to the classroom it is the one aspect of teaching that may fill you with dread and thoughts of will I be able to cope? This is hardly surprising given the images you may carry with you from your own school days or horror stories told by other trainees. Research also shows how pupil's misbehaviour can be linked to levels of stress, not only among trainees but also experienced teachers (Kyriacou and Sutcliffe, 1978; Chaplain, 2003). But remember that the fear is often worse than the reality. So, where do you begin with behaviour management?

Extended thinking

»   *Why is it fundamentally important that behaviour management is a key priority?*

»   *Who are you accountable to when behaviour management deteriorates?*

CASE STUDY

Introducing Stuart

A tutor is giving a tutorial prior to Stuart starting his placement. The tutor begins:

It is important that as soon as possible after arriving at your school, you ask for a copy of the school's behaviour policy. It is important that you also ask the class teacher about any specific behavioural issues that the class may have and what strategies are currently being employed to address them.

Critical questions

»   *Why is it important that Stuart asks for the school's behaviour policy?*

»   *Why should Stuart ask the class teacher if there are any specific behavioural issues?*

»   *Why is it important that Stuart finds out what behavioural strategies are currently being used in the class?*

Comment on Stuart's case study

By looking at the school's behaviour policy, Stuart will have an early opportunity to clearly understand the general principles of dealing with discipline and behaviour within his placement school. It will allow him an insight into what the school deems acceptable behaviour, what the hierarchy of sanctions and rewards are, and how they should be consistently used for positively promoting good behaviour. By Stuart asking if there are any specific behavioural issues in the class he will gain an insight into what issues he might have to face on a daily basis and if the behaviours he encounters are normal for that class or set of children. It is important that Stuart gets to know from the class teacher what the most effective strategies are for dealing with certain behaviours for any given child. This will mean he can be consistent in his use of behaviour management strategies, thereby maximising potential success when dealing with behaviour.

School behaviour policy

It is important that qualified teachers familiarise themselves with school policies but it is also essential that you as a trainee teacher request copies of key school documentation including the school's behaviour policy. Schools must have a behaviour policy (DfE, 2012a) and the head teacher is responsible, along with that of the governing body, for its establishment, development and implementation. It should outline the standard of behaviour expected of pupils, how this will be achieved, the school rules and the sanctions and rewards used. This policy should be freely available not only to parents and pupils but also to you as a trainee teacher. It provides a basis for a consistent approach to behaviour management in school and, for you, an invaluable source of advice on how a particular school will expect behaviours to be dealt with. By referencing this document you will gain an insight into what level of behaviour you as a class teacher will be required to deal with. It can serve to inform practice, help with strategies for the successful implementation of sanctions and rewards, as well as outlining the procedures you must follow if a more serious incident occurs. It will also help you know who must be involved so that the serious incident may be dealt with appropriately at a more senior level. The significance of a school's behaviour policy should not be underrated by anyone, as the House of Commons Education Committee (2011, page 25) suggest:

a good school behaviour policy, agreed and communicated to all staff, governors, pupils, parents and carers, consistently applied, is the basis of an effective approach to managing behaviour.

For you the school's behaviour policy will ultimately set the standard for the management of pupils' behaviour within your setting. It will provide you with a consistent and equitable application of the principles of behaviour management; give you valuable guidance on how issues such as playtime disputes may be dealt with should you be on duty; detail how children are expected to line up and how they should enter and leave school, etc.

Extended thinking

»   *Why do you think that school's behaviour policies can vary?*

»   *What element of a school's behaviour policy may be similar from school to school?*

Be prepared and make your mark

When you visit the classroom for the first time, pupils will be weighing you up to see if you are in control. Try not to be too friendly but always remember fostering positive relationships will be the key to a productive relationship. So it does not mean not talking to pupils but rather trying to convey an air of authority by giving good eye contact, using open, friendly gestures and being aware of your personal space and body language. Remember the first impression you make is long-lasting (Bar et al., 2006) so it is important you get it right from the off.

Take control

Behaviour for learning, as the term suggests, places a clear link between how children behave and how they learn. You need to realise that how you approach your lessons, for example, how they are planned, resourced and paced, will not only have an impact upon pupils' learning but also how pupils will behave. Therefore it is important that you see that good pupil behaviour will allow pupils to learn and make progress and it is just as much about what you do before the lessons begin as in the lesson itself.

You should be prepared in terms of your lesson planning, but also your resourcing needs and classroom organisation. In this way you are in control of the situation from the very start. Check you have all that you need for the lesson, that you have arranged the room as you require it, for example setting out tables for group work. All this will reduce your levels of anxiety and stress and signal to pupils that you know what you are doing. Make certain you are there to greet them on their arrival. Just by being around you will be able to regulate how pupils enter the classroom, guide them to the seats you want and be ready to signal that the lesson is about to begin.

Set clear rules

All lessons follow a similar pattern, for example you will have to introduce the topic, but only when you have the full attention of all of the children. The children may be aware of what to expect but they and you must be clear about the rules and routines that will be followed while they are in your care. By communicating clear boundaries to pupils, it will allow for the maximum engagement of pupils in the task in hand, thus promoting optimum opportunities for learning (McBer/DFES, 2000). Clear boundaries will also facilitate good relationships between you and the pupils and among the class as a whole.

Give ownership to the rules by creating them in consultation with your children. Find out from them what they feel is important and phrase the rules positively since this will have a more beneficial effect upon the children. Rather than listing things that cannot be done, for example 'Do not make unkind remarks to one another', phrase the rule so it is positive, for example 'Talk kindly to one another.' Also make rules short and few in number or the children and you will never remember them all. Display the rules prominently so that they can always be seen and therefore are always easily accessible and easily referred to by you and the class.

Have high expectations

You should have high expectations for behaviour as stated in Teachers' Standard 7 (DFE, 2011c). High expectations combined with clear strategies for pupil management will provide a sense of security, order and safety for pupils (McBer/DFES, 2000). For the majority of the time pupils' behaviours will not prove a challenge to you and you will rarely encounter the extremes of behaviour that you might have heard about. However, it is often low-level behavioural problems, such as a pupil annoying others, shouting out, wandering around the room, using tactics to avoid work, for example sharpening a pencil or going to the toilet, which will form the basis of continued frustration for you as a trainee teacher. So how might this be avoided?

In the classroom

Setting boundaries

You will find that when you first start teaching, children will initially listen quite politely, but it is as the lesson goes on, or in a future lesson, that children may listen less. You should try not to be too nervous in lessons and sound confident; remember, you are in control. You should take your time to speak slowly and clearly, use children's names, keeping eye contact in order to monitor the children's responses to you and your questions. You must quickly take on board class routines and establish them as your own in order that children know what is expected of them and what the codes of acceptable behaviour are. Children should listen politely to one another and not speak over you or others. At times you may have to remind them of this. Remember, if the children are talking then they will not be listening to you, and if this is the case they will be missing vital information and/or instructions. Remember to constantly model the behaviours you wish children to use in your classroom and remind them this is how you wish them to behave.

Asking questions

You will need to set the children guidelines for answering questions. For example, make it clear that you will not allow anyone to answer a question unless they have their hand up quietly. Explain that you have chosen a particular child because they put up their hand nicely. Remind children that they will not be chosen if they make too much noise when they put their hands up. You also should try and choose a variety of children to answer questions, not just those with their hands up. This will signal to other children that you are monitoring their engagement in the lessons and expecting everyone to participate. The use of lollipop sticks is a very good tactic in getting all pupils to engage (see Figure 5.1). It avoids over-eager children from 'popping', fidgeting and making silly noises due to their zeal to give their answer. It also encourages those children who do not volunteer to answer questions and usually keep their

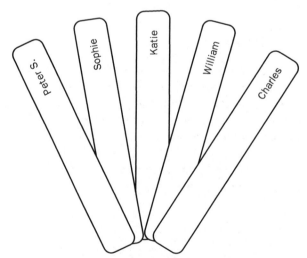

Figure 5.1 *Lollipop sticks for managing behaviour in whole-class teaching.*

hands well and truly in their laps. The strategy gives all pupils the opportunity to engage and interact in the lesson and to display more on-task behaviour. By now you are probably wondering what the lollipop strategy is. It is a simple behaviour management strategy that is easy to initiate within your own classroom. You need enough lollipop sticks for one per pupil. On one end of the lollipop stick you write the name of a child. Do this for each pupil in your class. Drop all the lollipop sticks into a pot (name end first). When you ask a question, instead of getting children to put their hands up, you draw one lollipop stick from the pot and read the name of the pupil who is going to answer the question.

Try to avoid looking at your notes and try to appear happy and relaxed when teaching or asking questions. If you need cues to remember what to say or have key points to make, you could write prompts or questions on the board or whiteboard slide prior to the lesson in order to help you maintain fluency.

Strategies for transitions

It is often when the children start moving on to a new task that you will find that behaviour might start to deteriorate. Consider the following case study:

CASE STUDY

Abhati's story

A tutor feeding back to Abhati after observing her lessons commented:

Though I felt the children made an attempt at completing your task, it took them too long to settle down and when you tried to get their attention the high level of noise meant that the children took too long to respond to your wish for them to be quiet. You seemed unaware of what was going on. There were a lot of children finding excuses to get out of their seats, for example to collect equipment, too much chatting and generally the children seemed quite uncertain about what you required of them. This meant they took too long to settle to the task set which wasted valuable time.

Critical questions

» *If you have already been on a placement, think about a time when you felt you lost the class's attention. Can you pinpoint where things went wrong? What could you have done differently?*

» *If you saw a pupil who was not on task, what might you ask them? How could you prompt them to resume their work?*

» *If the children are not listening, what strategies might you use to gain their attention? How might you verbally and non-verbally gain their attention?*

» *What might you do before the lesson starts and during the lesson to ensure pupils have few excuses to get up from their seats?*

Comment on Abhati's story

The problems Abhati encountered are not uncommon for trainee teachers, but they are easily avoided with some simple strategies.

- Position yourself so that all the children can see you and so that you can see them.

- Remember, if you are in the middle of the classroom you will not be able to see all around you: you should position yourself around the perimeter of the room for increased visibility.

- To gain children's attention try using a particular noise, eg ringing a bell, counting or clapping a sequence of sounds.

However, make certain that whatever strategy you use, the children know what it means and that you mean it.

For younger children you could use a puppet to signal when you are upset with them. Alternatively a puppet can be used as a positive reward and given to those you have spotted as being the fastest to become quiet. Sometimes you can signal that you wish them to be quiet by standing quietly and waiting for their attention. If this takes too long you could mention that next time they will be timed. The use of a sand-timer is very good for this, as children can physically see the time (sand) flowing which increases the sense of urgency among the class. It might be necessary to state that any additional time will come out of the children's break time. You could also employ non-verbal cues to show that they are keeping you waiting, eg folding your arms or looking at them in a disapproving manner.

To reduce pupils wishing to get out of their seats Abhati could, as part of her classroom routine, have made certain that the children had already got the items they needed out on their desks, therefore reducing the need for them to get up. She also needs to state where she wishes equipment and books to stay. If she is not clear, they will fiddle with items which will detract from the flow of her lesson. She should remember that preparation is key, including the need to check the state of equipment already used in school by other classes, eg ensuring that bulbs work, batteries have a charge and skipping ropes are not in a tangle.

Abhati should have verified that the class knew what it was doing, either by asking directly or by getting a child to repeat what has been said.

When you are new to the profession it will seem there is so much to remember but it will all become second nature with time. It is important for you to keep in mind that all those who seem proficient now have had similar issues and it is only with practice that you will achieve success. With good planning, preparation, the use of routines and classroom organisation you will be able to build success.

Inclusive teaching and learning

Given the inevitable diversity of abilities found within a class it is important that you clearly plan for inclusion. This will also reduce the likelihood of you experiencing inappropriate behaviours within a classroom. By the use of clear differentiation in terms of learning objectives, modifying your teaching styles to take account of the needs within your class, and by providing differentiated resources for children who find accessing learning difficult within the setting, you can allow children the opportunity to access learning rather than getting frustrated or bored while trying to complete a task. This will reduce the likelihood that children will then mess about in the lesson, causing you issues that could have been avoided from the offset.

Rewards and sanctions

It is important that alongside the strategies and routines outlined above you use a system of rewards and sanctions. These will reinforce good behaviour as well as signalling to pupils the deterrents that are in your arsenal for those who do not wish to comply.

Rewards

It is important that school rules link to the rewards and sanctions available in each setting (Steer, 2009). One of the most obvious ways of rewarding good work or behaviour is by the use of positive verbal praise. The children will know by the natural warmth by which it is given that you really mean it. Try to reward children as soon as they are being good when you first work with a class. You should pick specific positive elements to talk about when you praise a child or encourage other children to notice good behaviour, eg 'I like the way John quickly and quietly sat down at his desk'.

You will need to establish more tangible rewards systems for behaviour with the class as you establish rules and routines and a good working relationship with them. For individual children these may take the form of classroom rewards based around items such as house points, stars or stickers. However, do remember to also praise the child, commenting on why they were given this reward, so that it may serve to positively reinforce such behaviours in the future. You may also wish to establish golden time within your class. This allows pupils to build up a period of banked time when they behave well, or lose time off it if they misbehave. This time is then given back to them during the week in the form of an activity they value. You could also use raffle prizes to reward good behaviour, with a container being used to deposit raffle tickets which are given out when good behaviours are recognised. Whole class systems can also be established whereby you set up a container to put items such as marbles in every time the class as a whole behaves well, and this in turn can lead to a chosen reward by the class, such as extra break time. Whatever the reward, try to establish a means to record who has been honoured so that during the year a range of children in your class can be recognised. Also remember that rewards earned should not be taken away in anger. Children should keep what they justifiably earned through good behaviour and not have it wiped out through the course of one rash action.

Outside the classroom children can be recognised by you or other members of staff via praise assemblies. This is when school-based rewards may be issued, such as Citizen of the Week for kindness to others, or certificates for good behaviour. You as a class teacher can also award special privileges to those pupils who can be trusted both in the classroom and outside of your sight. They may include jobs such as house point monitors, recycling monitors and children who collect items from the office. If you are particularly pleased with a child you can always send them to the head teacher who will in turn support your praise by issuing his or her own reward.

In addition to the rewards issued at school it is good practice to involve parents in sharing in pupils' successes by sending home tangible signs of rewards. Though we often involve parents in issues related to sanctions it is important that the positives are shared as well. They may often provide an important bridge for you when times get tougher and demonstrate to parents that you are equally supportive of the child whatever their behaviour might be.

Sanctions

Sometimes no matter how positive you are and how positively you seek to reward behaviour, you will find that some sort of sanction may be needed to maintain discipline in class or to continue to motivate pupils.

Schools use a range of sanctions. Examples, listed in increasing severity, are removing privileges, keeping pupils in at break time, finishing work (detentions), contacting parents, temporary exclusions (a period of time that a child is not allowed to attend the school) or in the most severe of cases a permanent exclusion (banning the child from attending their school). It is important, as Arthur and Cremin (2010) suggest; that whatever the sanction or reward system used it must be fit for purpose and be based around items that are not liked by the pupils.

It is important, however, at this point for you to remember that sanctions for some children will have little impact if used too often. Sometimes some children's behaviour may not improve when sanctions are applied since they feed off the negative attention that sanctions provide. At times, therefore, remember that tactical ignoring of misbehaviour may prove the best option, especially given the bigger battle you may have to fight later on.

Whatever system of sanctions you decide to use it must be in line with the school's behaviour policy. This is something that you must find and read at the very beginning of your practice so that you are aware of the school's agreed and consistent approach not only to using sanctions but also for rewarding behaviour too. However, after you have read this policy it is up to you to consider whether your use of sanctions is appropriate given the level of misdemeanour and the age of the child, and if they will have any influence on a child if they are carried out. For children to respond to any sanction it must be something they will not like doing or having withdrawn from them in the school day. It is hard when you first start in a school to know this sort of information, but do ask colleagues for their opinions and views. Sanctions might involve placing a child's name on the board, removing house points, moving them in the class or depriving them of some activity or break time. It is also important that you remind children that a particular sanction is being used because of the behaviour they have exhibited. Tell the child that you like them but you do not like the behaviour and that is why they are in trouble. Also, whatever the child has done always try to start afresh once the sanction has been carried out. If you are not careful your relationship with the child could easily enter a negative downward spiral. Consider the following case study:

CASE STUDY

Christos' story

Christos is receiving feedback on an observation made by his class teacher regarding a specific behaviour he encountered in the class:

I think the majority of the lesson went well apart from the incident I witnessed with Simon which was quite worrying. I was surprised he didn't tear his page out. I know you wanted him to stop drawing on the page but you seemed to be getting agitated when telling him off just because he wasn't doing what you wished. It almost felt like a battle of wills. You said if he continued drawing on the page rather than starting again on a fresh page he would have to stay in at break time. You said that time and time again but it didn't really seem to be making any difference. You then started taking house points off too. However, when it was time for them to go out he left without doing what you wanted since you didn't appear to know what to do.

Critical questions

» Outline and explain the problems with Christos' approach to this situation.

» How could Christos have dealt with this situation more effectively?

» Who could you seek help from if you felt you could not deal with such a situation?

Comment on Christos' story

In this situation Christos was getting agitated so it is likely that he would say things that he had not thought through and might regret. He needed to remove himself from the situation during the incident in order to think calmly through his approach and to mentally rehearse his use of non-confrontational language to be used in the situation. He should have started by trying to ascertain if there was an issue with understanding or accessing the task that made Simon do what he was doing before issuing sanctions. Christos then made the classic mistakes of building up more than one sanction and not following through with them. He should have told the child only once what would happen and made it clear to the child it was his choice either to do as Christos wished or stay in. Christos should have said, I know you can make the right choice and congratulated Simon at the end of the lesson if he had complied. Christos could have then pointed out that by making the right choice he could go out. Christos should not have started using alternative sanctions; the initial sanction should have been enough. All that happened was it signalled to Simon Christos' desperation and Simon leaving the room meant that Christos' authority had been undermined for the future.

Do not feel that you always have to issue sanctions for negative behaviours. Remember at times it may be prudent to tactically ignore behaviours if they are insignificant or if they prove inconsequential in the grand scheme of behaviours from a particular child. If you do not do this you will find you are always on at a particular child, which is not good for any relationship.

Sometimes a child's behaviour is the result of them craving attention from others or yourself, so try to ignore the behaviour in the hope that it will diminish or even cease. If this does not happen, remove the child from their audience, for example by asking them to move seats or if necessary even sending them to another place which you have agreed.

Extended thinking

»   *What, for you, are the five most important strategies for managing behaviour?*

»   *Rank them and suggest reasons for your choices.*

When class-based sanctions are not enough

It may be that despite your best efforts at modifying a behaviour it persists. In this case you may have to involve the class teacher for help and guidance. One course of action is that you, with your teacher, will talk to the parent about the issue and between you draw up an agreed course of action based around sanctions and rewards. In some situations, however, despite the consistent use of rewards and sanctions, interventions from you and the class teacher and liaison with parents, you may only achieve minor modifications to the undesirable behaviours of a child. This may be due to a child's very specific behavioural issues and these in turn will need careful management. This may be enough for them to remain in school and for you to successfully teach them and others in the classroom. If this is the case you will probably have to constantly work at building up trust and rapport with such a child in an attempt to remain on a positive footing with them.

Extreme behaviours

In rare cases class-based sanctions will not be enough to manage extremes of behaviours rooted in special educational needs, poor self-esteem, neglect or violence in the home along with poor rates of school attendance. Such lack of respect for authority and extreme negative behaviours will become whole-school issues and, if not resolvable, will lead to the risk of either temporary or permanent exclusion. But what happens then to such children?

In such cases most pupils will attend a pupil referral unit (PRU) which under section 19 of the Education Act 1996 exists to provide education to children who are of compulsory school age who are unable to attend a maintained school for reasons of illness, exclusion or other reasons. It is the local authority's responsibility for arranging suitable education for permanently excluded pupils (DfE 2013a).

Due to a change in government legislation from 1 September 2012, it is now possible for you to undertake a teaching practice or carry out your NQT year in a PRU. Despite the challenging nature of such children, you will, as in other mainstream placements, be allowed an opportunity to teach a balanced curriculum. At a PRU this will include mathematics, English, science, PSHE, ICT and careers guidance and education (DfES, 2005). Such a placement will offer you an opportunity to be involved in teaching children with special educational needs or statements linked to emotional and behavioural difficulties. Alongside the staff who work at such centres you will be trained to respond to children's needs and not only have to deal with the challenges they bring but also their erratic attendance rates, since many of the children often attend such centres unplanned and mid-term (Brown, 2011). You will be involved in assessing children's needs and offering wherever possible a personalised programme of support and education, since you will need to be responsive to the difficult behavioural issues such children pose. This work is very fulfilling and may mean that children have the capacity to return to mainstream settings or can progress to further education or employment. For some children, despite their emotional issues, with improvements in their behaviour, they can often achieve good academic standards. Surely this is something that we should aspire to in our education system and that you may be keen to be involved in during your future career.

Extended thinking

» *What factors might need to be taken into account when managing behaviour?*

» *Is it appropriate for all children to remain in the mainstream given a range of behaviours?*

» *What are your absolute boundaries children must cross for you to seek help when managing their behaviour?*

Chapter reflections

Getting your behaviour management strategies right is the key to enhancing pupils' learning. Take time to observe other teachers in order to identify behaviour management strategies that you can add to your toolkit. Having a rich armoury in terms of behaviour strategies will stand you in good stead as you will often have to change your strategy to suit individuals or different classes. Ensure that you are consistent in your approach to discipline and you should establish respect and trust from the children in your class.

Critical points

» *Read and follow the school's behaviour policy.*

» *Quickly establish rules and routines and link them to rewards and sanctions.*

» *Be consistent and mean what you say.*

» *Remember to find time to listen to pupils to understand why they are behaving the way they are.*

» *It is the behaviour you do not like and not the child.*

Taking it further

Arthur J and Cremin, T (eds) (2010) *Learning to Teach in the Primary School.* London: Routledge.

Canter, L (2010) *Assertive Discipline: Positive Behaviour Management for Today's Classroom.* Bloomington, IN: Solution Tree Press.

Rogers, B (2007) *Behaviour Management: A Whole School Approach.* London: Paul Chapman.

Rogers, B (2011) *Classroom Behaviour.* London: Sage.

Rogers, B and McPherson, E (2008) *Behaviour Management with Young Children: Crucial First Steps with Children 3–7 Years.* London: Sage.

Steer, A (2009) *Learning Behaviour: Lessons Learned. A Review of Behavioural Standards and Practices in Our Schools.* Nottingham: DCSF Publications.

6 Planning and assessment

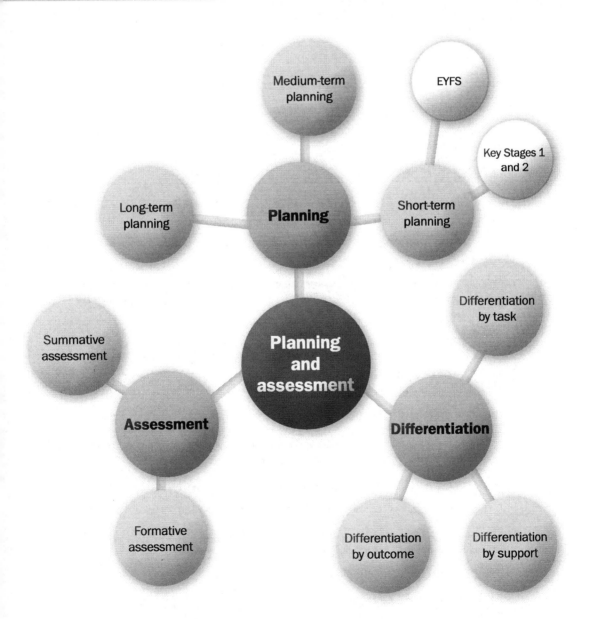

Teachers' Standards (DfE, 2011c)

1 Set high expectations which inspire, motivate and challenge pupils

- set goals that stretch and challenge pupils of all backgrounds, abilities and dispositions.

2 Promote good progress and outcomes by pupils

- be accountable for pupils' attainment, progress and outcomes
- be aware of pupils' capabilities and their prior knowledge, and plan teaching to build on these
- demonstrate knowledge and understanding of how pupils learn and how this impacts on teaching.

4 Plan and teach well-structured lessons

- promote a love of learning and children's intellectual curiosity
- reflect systematically on the effectiveness of lessons and approaches to teaching
- contribute to the design and provision of an engaging curriculum within the relevant subject area(s).

5 Adapt teaching to respond to the strengths and needs of all pupils

- know when and how to differentiate appropriately, using approaches which enable pupils to be taught effectively
- have a secure understanding of how a range of factors can inhibit pupils' ability to learn, and how best to overcome these
- demonstrate an awareness of the physical, social and intellectual development of children, and know how to adapt teaching to support pupils' education at different stages of development
- have a clear understanding of the needs of all pupils, including those with special educational needs; those of high ability; those with English as an additional language; those with disabilities; and be able to use and evaluate distinctive teaching approaches to engage and support them.

6 Make accurate and productive use of assessment

- know and understand how to assess the relevant subject and curriculum areas, including statutory assessment requirements
- make use of formative and summative assessment to secure pupils' progress
- use relevant data to monitor progress, set targets and plan subsequent lessons
- give pupils regular feedback, both orally and through accurate marking, and encourage pupils to respond to the feedback.

8 Fulfil wider professional responsibilities

- deploy support staff effectively.

Introduction

While on placement you may be mainly concerned with the nuts and bolts of teaching and your ability to survive the frenetic pace at which you have to plan. Getting your planning spot on is of course imperative; however, the part assessment plays should not be underestimated as it is key to your ability to pitch lessons appropriately.

This chapter covers the interconnectedness of the two elements, planning and assessment, and the part they have to play in pupils' learning. Various levels of planning are presented, ie long-term, medium-term and short-term, and you are asked to consider the purpose of each. The chapter also looks at the place and purpose of differentiation. Informing all planning (whether it is in the EYFS or later key stages) are the two main assessment types – formative and summative.

Planning

When you are first given responsibility for your new class you will need to plan a curriculum to meet their learning needs. Remember that this forms part of the continuous process of learning, as shown in Figure 6.1.

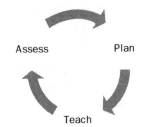

Assess   Plan

Teach

Figure 6.1 _The continuous process of learning._

You need to make sure you know who to talk to about the school's planning process. Find out what the long-term planning and medium-term planning look like for a particular curricular area, not only for your class but also in terms of how it might fit into the progression of learning for this subject across the school. You can then think about how individual pupils might be taught within this framework.

Long-term planning

Long-term planning is generally outlined in the school's policy documents, which can be accessed through the subject co-ordinator, head teacher or in most cases by asking the school secretary. This planning has been developed with reference to government publications such as the national curriculum (DfE, 2013b) and the statutory framework for the Early Years Foundation Stage (DfE, 2014c) documents. Though such guidance will outline the content of the curriculum, it will not tell individual schools how this might be taught. Therefore a school's long-term planning is likely to have been developed through what was no doubt a lengthy process of staff-based discussions. This will certainly have been carried out before your arrival and will have involved a detailed discussion around the appropriate placing of units of knowledge for best effect.

The school's long-term planning will relate to the statutory content of the programmes of study and each key stage, and it will tell you:

- what the school curriculum is and how it is to be covered;
- how the curriculum is organised across the key stages and year groups;
- any time allocations that may be attached to each unit of study.

Medium-term planning

Medium-term planning comes out of the school's long-term planning and is much more specific in its nature, with specific detail for each subject or topic covered through half-termly or termly plans. It covers:

- the learning objectives for your class;
- the knowledge, skills and methods that need to be taught;
- how the knowledge, skills and methods might be chunked for progression.

Though it is not statutory, a large majority of schools tend to adopt published schemes or the government's schemes of work on which to base their medium-term planning. Such strategies enable schools to group objectives in a meaningful way and secure progression in learning. However, this does not mean that they should be adopted without adaptation, and you will need to tailor the learning to each cohort of children you will have.

As a trainee teacher you will not be left on your own to struggle with what might feel a very daunting task. Remember that you can seek help and advice from your mentor, the school subject co-ordinator and other class teachers.

Short-term planning

Short-term planning is the means by which you adapt the broad objectives outlined in the medium-term plan into a daily class plan for delivering learning which will allow you to devise engaging and meaningful lessons. However, it is important for you to note that it is the role of differentiation (outlined later in this chapter) to adapt what you have planned into tasks and activities that will cater for the range of needs within your class.

When you first start teaching short-term planning will feel quite a chore, but it provides you with a means to mentally rehearse what you are going to teach, and the order in which you might do things, alongside the resourcing necessary for the lesson. Short-term plans also provide a permanent record of what you have taught for your head teacher, mentor or in the event of an Ofsted inspection. However, with regard to Ofsted it is important to note:

Inspectors will not expect to find a particular model or format for planning: they are more interested in the impact of planning on your teaching and the children's learning (DfES, 2003, page 78).

Short-term planning can be an excellent reference source for a TA who may be assigned to the class you are teaching. Before you embark upon planning for any aspect of a child's learning it is vitally important that you get to know the pupils for whom you are planning work so that any learning objectives may be met. When you first meet a class try and gather as much information as possible about the children.

CASE STUDY

Introducing Alima

In January Alima was placed with a Year 4 mixed-ability group of pupils. She was given the school's history policy and a copy of the Year 4 history medium-term plan. Alima wondered what on earth to do next and how she would tackle such a challenge, having never planned weekly history-specific lessons before and certainly not for this mixed-ability Year 4 class.

Critical questions

»   *Who might Alima approach in order to find out more about how history is taught in the school?*

»   *Where or from whom in the school might Alima start to get an idea of the ability ranges/learning needs she might face when delivering these lessons?*

»   *How might she start to gather information about the resources needed to successfully develop her lessons?*

Comment on Alima's story

You, like Alima, will not be alone in this task. Alima could talk to other class teachers, the subject co-ordinator and her mentor to help her start to understand the teaching of history in her placement school. She needs to find out about the pupil tracking system used within the school and use this system to start to build up a profile of the pupils in her class, to include the less and more able. Alima could supplement her knowledge of these pupils by talking to the SENCO.

Short-term planning formats will vary according to your training college or the school placement setting. They will also vary with each key stage, ie Early Years Foundation Stage (EYFS) and Key Stages 1 and 2.

EYFS

For the EYFS short-term planning is generally based around the long-term planning. It is largely derived from informal assessments and the observations you make of particular children and in consultation with other practitioners and/or parents. Planning for the EYFS is all about a child's next steps in learning, with the learning intentions being linked to the stepping stones or early learning goals appropriate for the stage of development of that child. EYFS planning is linked to the seven areas of learning (DfE, 2014). These include the three prime areas of communication and language, physical development and personal, social and emotional development. These prime areas are strengthened and promoted through the four other areas of literacy, maths, understanding the world and expressive art and design. Practitioners who have the youngest children who are not yet ready for school are expected to concentrate on the three prime areas. However as the children grow in confidence and ability in these three prime areas of development a more equal focus on all areas of learning should be given. Planning should provide for purposeful play, alongside a combination of adult-led and child-initiated activities. You will need to include how you organise the children, the resourcing, how activities are adapted to match pupils' needs and the range of activities to be employed. Your planning should also be mindful of the characteristics of effective teaching and learning at this age. This includes, playing and exploring, active learning and creating and thinking critically.

You might also consider how observations may be carried out.

Key Stages 1 and 2

With younger children it is more likely that you will plan for the core subjects of literacy and numeracy separately and that other foundation subjects will be integrated through topics. However, on occasions you may find that as you plan for older children, the core along with other foundation subjects may represent separate elements of your planning. How you plan for subjects in the curriculum will depend entirely on your school setting. For example, some schools will plan for separate subjects and others may take a 'Mantle of the Expert' curriculum design approach to planning. (If you want to learn more about this approach to curriculum design, see the Taking it further section at the end of this chapter.) A good weekly planning format will:

- identify key learning objectives to be covered and link to related curriculum documents;

- build on prior knowledge;

- identify success criteria;

- highlight any cross-curricular links;

- stipulate resources and ICT to be used;

- detail a clear structure and timings for the lesson;

- state the activities/tasks to be covered;

- provide a summary of different activities linked to differentiation;

- state how the TA will be deployed;

- include key vocabulary to be used within the lesson.

From reading Chapter 1, you know that you are expected to reflect on your practice continually. Part of this reflective process is your ability to evaluate the lessons you have taught. This evaluation is a key part of planning and it will allow you to develop your teaching through self-evaluation and critical reflection. It is important that you analyse your performance in terms of how things went and how well pupils learnt in order that you may seek future improvements in your performance. Good evaluation will also allow you to link children's prior attainment to how you wish to develop future learning. Your evaluation may take the form of a formal written piece that may be an entry in your PDP, professional dialogue with your mentor, or merely, but most efficiently and effectively, annotation of your lesson plans.

Differentiation

Differentiation is a term you will have encountered throughout your university training and through literature such as DCSF (2008a). You may have also heard it related to the idea of personalised learning, which is also linked to tailoring learning to children's needs, interests and abilities (DfES, 2006b). Differentiation should be part of your good inclusive practice. It allows you to accommodate and challenge the range of pupils in your care so that they have the best chance of accessing and developing their learning whatever their age or ability. In essence differentiation is about matching a task or activity to a child's specific skills, knowledge, interests and experiences. This may include, for example, pupils who have:

- a specific learning difficulty;
- physical/medical difficulties;
- English as an additional language (EAL).

Good differentiation is one of the key components of outstanding teaching and is probably one of the greatest challenges you will face. How will you successfully differentiate given the wide-ranging, mixed levels of ability and learning styles within your classroom? To differentiate too little will mean that you will fail to allow all children to successfully access learning; too much and you will face the issue of overloading yourself with work. In order to balance this commitment there are three possible ways you can differentiate learning:

- differentiation by task;
- differentiation by support;
- differentiation by outcome.

The combined use of these three strategies will help you gain control of what may seem an overwhelming task.

Critical questions

»   *What do you understand differentiation by task to mean?*

»   *What do you think differentiation by support might involve?*

»   *What do you understand by the term differentiation by outcome?*

Differentiation by task

Differentiation by task involves setting different tasks dependent upon the abilities of the pupils. It might involve creating a specific investigation or worksheet which caters for a particular need. For example:

- the level of English used has been made simpler to comprehend or reduced in length;
- it employs a cloze procedure, asking pupils to complete sentences using identified key words;
- images are used to aid comprehension;
- more practical-based activities are encouraged to help pupils access the curriculum.

In order to maximise the effectiveness of this strategy you can group children to complete the same task given their similar needs. Read Nathan's account below of an observation he made when watching another class teacher (Monique) teaching English and mathematics one morning.

CASE STUDY

Nathan's statement

I was observing Monique teaching English and maths. The university's expectation is that I have to observe other teachers as much as possible so as to inform my own practice. I was intrigued by how Monique organised her classroom. Pupils sat in the same place for their maths and English lessons. I asked her whether the pupils were organised according to their ability or if she'd allowed them to sit with their friends for both lessons. Monique said that it made her life much easier by sitting them in the same places and the children likewise weren't confused by constantly moving around the classroom. At first I thought this was sensible but subsequently I have started to question Monique's practice.

Critical questions

»   *Why are Monique's reasons for arranging pupils in her class unsatisfactory?*

»   *What potential impact might this practice have on pupil outcomes?*

»   *What would you do if you were a trainee teacher in Monique's class?*

Reducing workload is never a valid or viable reason for how you position children in your class. A grouping may only last for that one activity or be linked to a specific area of the curriculum. What should always be at the forefront of your mind is what the children can gain from the activity and if the class organisation suits their learning needs.

Differentiation by support

This involves you targeting the class-based support that you may have within the classroom. This could include a TA or another adult who may be in the class on a less frequent basis. You might use them to work on a task with children in order to:

*   read sections of print that the child might find difficult to comprehend on their own;

*   help support a child with a practical-based activity to aid comprehension;

*   act as a scribe for a child to help speed up their work rate.

Differentiation by outcome

This involves setting open-ended tasks which allow pupils to work at their own pace. Though initially this may seem the best solution for you, it is not always considered good practice when used on a regular basis. It can leave children to their own devices due to a lack of challenge, and pupils may do only a limited amount of work because the requirements are not defined.

Extended thinking

» *What are the key sources of information needed when planning for a class?*

» *How might you support the range of need in your planning so children's needs can be met?*

Assessment

So what is assessment and how does it help to inform planning, teaching and ultimately learning? Assessment involves deciding what evidence you will collect in order to formulate a judgement about pupil learning and attainment. The period of assessment will vary. You will be expected to assess within a lesson against particular learning objectives but also over a protracted period of time, for example at the end of a unit of work or term. You should ask yourself if the assessment will lead to improved learning and teaching. Fundamentally, if the assessments you conduct do not feed into your planned learning cycle for the pupils then the process becomes a pointless exercise.

Assessment comes in many guises but the two main types are formative and summative. The two are used with similar aims in mind, that of enhancing pupil learning and subsequent attainment; however, they are carried out at differing points.

Formative assessment

Formative assessment is ongoing assessment conducted by you before and throughout every lesson. Before commencing a new topic, for example, you should ascertain what level of prior knowledge the class has in order to plan appropriately. Formative assessment is undertaken minute by minute as you ask the class questions and listen to pupil responses. The information you glean from the pupils' answers should inform your teaching. You should adapt planned lessons based on the acquisition of the knowledge you witness in the pupil responses. If pupils are giving incorrect answers or are reluctant to respond, they are probably struggling to grasp the new knowledge you are imparting. As you assess the children during a lesson you should be flexible in your teaching and move away from your planned lesson in order to address any problems children are having. Likewise you may realise that the class has understood a concept much quicker than you anticipated. Again you should deviate from your planning in order to extend and challenge your pupils.

Assessment for learning (AfL) is one aspect of formative assessment that you will witness in action while you are on placement. In 2002 the Assessment Reform Group (DCSF, 2008c) defined assessment for learning as:

... the process of seeking and interpreting evidence for use by pupils and their teachers to decide where the pupils are in their learning, where they need to go and how best to get there.

The ten principles for assessment for learning guide classroom practice, which should:

1. be part of effective planning;

2. be focused on how students learn;

3. be central to classroom practice;

4.   be a key professional skill;

5.   be sensitive and constructive;

6.   foster motivation;

7.   promote understanding of goals and criteria;

8.   help pupils know how to improve;

9.   develop the pupils' capacity for self-assessment;

10.   recognise all educational achievement.

You should therefore strive to develop a toolkit of creative AfL strategies including the use of photographs and sticky notes to record children's successes. Formative assessment or AfL should inform your next planning, learning and teaching cycle. It focuses on the knowledge pupils have gained and how they assimilate this understanding in a variety of contexts. In 2004 the government of the day heightened the profile of assessment for learning through the release of their 'Excellence and Enjoyment' (DfES, 2004) materials. Clear AfL characteristics were defined along with ten key AfL principles (see Taking it further for more information). Assessment for learning, when used most effectively with pupils, has the potential to raise standards and meet the needs of each individual. So when are you likely to use AfL strategies?

You should seek to use AfL strategies on a day-to-day basis as they are fundamental to your success as a teacher and the fostering of independent pupils. Sally's narrative describes how she delivered a maths lesson in Year 3. Read the narrative and then reflect on which AfL strategies she employed.

CASE STUDY

Sally's Year 3 maths lesson

All children were on the carpet and I started with a warm-up related to the five times table. Each time I asked a question the children wrote their answers on a small individual whiteboard and, on cue, they showed me their answers. I asked my TA to make a note of those who had got it right/wrong on sticky notes for me so that I had a record at the end of the lesson. I then moved on to telling the time. I shared the learning objective with the class and then proceeded to demonstrate how to tell the time for five past, ten past the hour, etc. and differentiated my questions according to ability. I then showed some big clocks on the IWB (interactive whiteboard) one after another. The children had some time cards (from which to select) that matched the clock faces. On some occasions I asked the children to speak to their talk partner before showing me their answers and sometimes I asked them to show me immediately. I then went on to explain the pupil activities and asked the children to show me thumbs up, down or in the middle to indicate how confident they felt before they went off to their tables. I made a mental note to myself and went to check on some of those that had struggled in the beginning or lacked confidence. Working in pairs, a child in each pair sequenced a set of card clocks. I then asked the observer in the pair to mark their partner's sequence and give feedback. Children then presented the clock faces they'd drawn to match certain times and the other children in the class gave two stars and a wish.

At the end of the lesson I instructed the pupils to draw at the end of their work a smiley face, straight face or sad face in relation to the learning objective and success criteria. I then took in their work and marked it. Having marked the work and given developmental written feedback, I realised that I had about half a dozen who were still struggling and noted their names on my planning sheet.

Critical questions

» List the AfL strategies that Sally used in the maths lesson.

» In what way did the AfL strategies inform Sally of each individual's progress?

» Having identified that some of the children were still finding it difficult to tell the time to the nearest five minutes, what could Sally do to address this in the next lesson? List your suggestions.

Comment on Sally's story

Sally undoubtedly has a good understanding of AfL strategies as she employed a range in her teaching. The use of small whiteboards and the time cards enabled the effectively deployed TA to assess and take notes on those achieving or otherwise. These assessments could then be fed back to the teacher. Use of differentiated and key probing questions enabled Sally to test out the individuals' and the pairs of pupils' understanding (teacher assessment). By using non-verbal pupil responses, eg thumbs and smiley faces, Sally was able to identify those who were in need of additional support and monitor them throughout the lesson (self-assessment). Through the pair activity towards the end of the lesson pupils evaluated each other's success or failure and gave stars and a wish (peer assessment). Writing developmental feedback on children's work is always helpful but you need to ensure that it relates to the learning objective and that pupils are given the opportunity the following day to review their comments and improve their work. In addition, to ensure that the assessments were purposeful Sally annotated her plans and used her comments to inform her next lesson. In particular Sally completely reorganised the groups in her class for the next lesson, putting those that had struggled on one table with her so that she could reframe their learning and address the misconceptions that had arisen the previous day.

Summative assessment

Summative assessment sums up the learning. It can occur at the end of a sequence of lessons, or even at the end of the term, year or key stage. Outcomes from the assessments, which are more often than not formal in nature, can be used to set future targets. You could for example take results from the Early Years Foundation Stage Profile (DfE, 2014), statutory assessment tests (SATs) and optional tests and use them to inform a sequence of lessons and future learning. Alternatively you might share the outcomes of the tests with the next year group's class teacher so as to inform medium-term planning. From your analysis of a variety of tests, you may (with others in the school) identify emerging themes and this could inform curriculum design in the long term.

There are two main summative assessments that you are likely to encounter while on placement:

•   assessment of learning (AoL);

•   assessing pupils' progress (APP).

Assessment of learning assesses the learning that has occurred and as such you should be conscious of the fact that any formal testing should properly assess the full range of learning aims within a given time frame. SATs, for example, may not cover all areas or concepts that you might teach in a given year. You may observe the execution of SATs or optional tests while you are on placement. In the study below Bethan describes what she witnessed on her third week on placement.

CASE STUDY

Bethan's SAT baptism

I had been at the school for three weeks and all I had seen in Year 6 was teaching to the test. Every day the teacher would give them another question from an English paper. Day in, day out, the routine was always the same. I wondered if it was always like this. On the Monday of the third week, I arrived in school and couldn't believe what I was seeing. All the displays had been either taken down or covered up with large sheets of paper. The tables had been pulled apart and chairs placed at either end so as to separate the pupils as much as possible. Then the children arrived. The look of astonishment on their faces was dreadful. Nothing could have prepared them for the scene that presented itself that morning. For half of the pupils in the class, things were going to get even worse as they were chaperoned into the hall. A huge expanse of space with tables and chairs distributed in neat long lines lay before me. Then the test started. I was acting as an invigilator and some of the children started to cry.

Critical questions

»   *Based on the study, how effective do you think tests were in ascertaining the level of attainment of each pupil? Give reasons for your response.*

»   *What would you do if presented with a similar situation?*

»   *Why do you think schools function like this?*

»   *What are the positive and negative aspects to AfL and AoL?*

Assessing pupils' progress (APP) is a teacher assessment but one that is summative in nature. It is a structured approach to in-school assessment. You may find that you are involved in APP meetings and you should fully engage with the process. Judgements can on occasions be subjective and you should be prepared to enter into lengthy professional dialogues and provide evidence to support your assertions relating to individual pupil attainment. APP processes will enable you to identify the next steps in learning for pupils. In addition you will be able to employ APP so as to:

- draw conclusions about how well or otherwise your pupils attain;

- refine, hone, enhance and develop your understanding of the subject and progression within it;

- identify the strengths and weaknesses of individual pupils and the wider cohort that you teach via a diagnostic tool;

- track pupils' progress over time;

- inform you how to develop curriculum planning;

- facilitate and set developmental targets that you can share with both pupils and parents;

- appropriately match teaching to individual needs;

- support transitions, for example from Key Stage 1 to 2, by means of providing quality-assured information at key points;

- enhance existing arrangements.

APP covers reading, writing, speaking and listening and mathematics. Try to find out when your mentor and school staff are involved in these meetings so that you can play an active role in the assessment practices of the school and assist in the moderating of colleagues' verdicts.

Extended thinking

» *When might formative and summative means of assessment be best deployed?*

» *How might you tailor assessments to best inform your teaching?*

Chapter reflections

Assessment should be the keystone to your planned teaching and learning cycles. Rather than coming last in the process of planning and delivery, it should be the bedrock of all your teaching. Without efficient and effective assessment strategies, you will fail to develop exemplary lesson plans that are personalised, cater for the learning needs of all pupils and foster pupil independence.

Critical points

» *Use all three types of differentiation to accommodate the variety of learning styles.*

» *Embrace short-term planning!*

» *Develop a toolkit of creative assessment strategies.*

» *Value the importance and place of assessment within the teaching and learning cycle.*

» *Do not equate assessment with testing – but use the full range of strategies to inform your assessment of pupils.*

Taking it further

Association for Achievement and Improvement through Assessment. www.aaia.org.uk/afl/assessment-reform-group/.

Mantle of the Expert. www.mantleoftheexpert.com/about-moe/introduction/.

7 Teaching the core curriculum

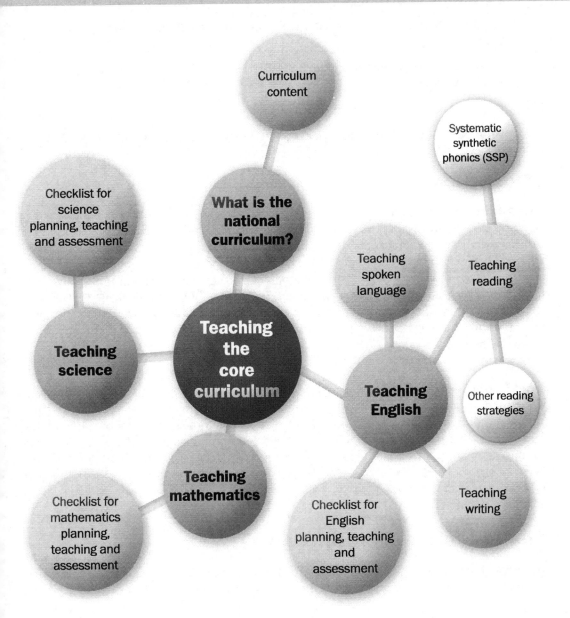

Teachers' Standards (DfE, 2011c)

3 Demonstrate good subject and curriculum knowledge

- have a secure knowledge of the relevant subject(s) and curriculum areas, foster and maintain pupils' interest in the subject and address misunderstandings

- demonstrate a critical understanding of developments in the subject and curriculum areas, and promote the value of scholarship

- demonstrate an understanding of and take responsibility for promoting high standards of literacy, articulacy and the correct use of standard English, whatever the teacher's specialist subject

- if teaching early reading, demonstrate a clear understanding of systematic synthetic phonics

- if teaching early mathematics, demonstrate a clear understanding of appropriate teaching strategies.

4 Plan and teach well-structured lessons

- contribute to the design and provision of an engaging curriculum within the relevant subject area(s).

Introduction

Since 1989 community primary schools in England have been required to teach the national curriculum, a statutory framework which was designed to provide pupils *with an introduction to the essential knowledge that they need to be educated citizens* (DfE, 2013b) across a range of agreed subjects. This chapter seeks to enhance your understanding of the curriculum, in particular the core subjects of English, mathematics and science. It is important to note that the national curriculum is *just one element in the education of every child* (DfE, 2013b) and is only statutory in state-maintained schools, although all schools in England must publish their individual curriculum online. It is worth spending some time researching the historical context of the national curriculum in England in order to understand the rationale behind its development.

In order to reflect upon your own subject knowledge and be able to demonstrate your understanding it is important that you understand how the national curriculum (DfE, 2013b) is laid out, its aims and values, but also its limitations. This chapter introduces you to the current programmes of study for English, mathematics and science (ibid); it also demonstrates how these build upon the principles of the statutory framework for the Early Years Foundation Stage (EYFS) (DfE, 2014c). You are given the opportunity to critically reflect on the progression of learning within each core curriculum area and on what makes an effective teaching experience.

What is the national curriculum?

The national curriculum (DfE, 2013b) applies to pupils of compulsory school age in maintained schools (ie schools that are government-funded via a local authority). It is organised on the basis of four key stages. The primary curriculum deals with Key Stage 1 and Key Stage 2 (Years 1–6). In addition there is a mandatory framework for Early Years practitioners working with children aged 0–5, which provides the expected entitlements and standards for those teaching in nursery or reception classrooms.

While it is important that you are aware of and adhere to the mandatory frameworks and statutory guidance, it is equally important to remember that your role as a professional teacher actually requires you to interpret and make sense of the documentation. Only then can you plan creative, engaging ways to implement the curriculum. Published resources and schemes of work for subjects you are less knowledgeable about can be useful, but should not become a substitute for your understanding of progression and curriculum content.

Curriculum content

The curriculum has been structured in the same way since its inception, with English, mathematics and science identified as core subjects and the rest of the curriculum areas labelled as foundation subjects. Each subject of the national curriculum (ibid) has a programme of study which details the content, skills and processes to be taught across the key stages and sets the required standard for knowledge and understanding within the subject. While there is no longer a nationally agreed set of Attainment Targets, it is stated that *By the end of each key stage, pupils are expected to know, apply and understand matters, skills and processes specified in the relevant programme of study* (DfE, 2013b): it is up to individual schools to decide how best to ascertain this. (NB Sample assessment materials for English, mathematics and science can be found at https://www.gov.uk/government/collections/national-curriculum-assessments-2016-sample-materials) Figure 7.1 demonstrates how these elements of the curriculum are intended to be viewed, with the programme of study sitting within a wider body of subject-specific knowledge to provide teachers with the

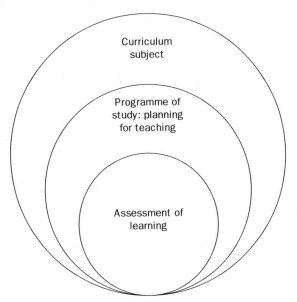

Curriculum
subject

Programme of
study: planning
for teaching

Assessment of
learning

Figure 7.1 *The links between aspects of the national curriculum (DfE, 2013b)*

necessary guidance for planning minimum coverage of the subject, and assessment linked directly to the intended coverage to enable accurate evaluation of pupils' learning.

The curriculum outlines which aspects of the subject should be taught *across a key stage* and details in which year (or age phase in Key Stage 2) children should encounter new knowledge. The programmes of study are split into *Statutory requirements, Notes and guidance (non-statutory),* with additional appendices and glossaries for English and mathematics.

As an initial teacher trainee you are in the fortunate position of being able to use the existing curriculum maps, topic webs and other mid-term planning formats already prepared by your mentor in school. Should this not be the case, however, you should spend some time considering how you would organise appropriate coverage of the curriculum across a year or age phase to ensure logical progression and subject development.

Critical questions

Using the latest curriculum documentation, consider the following questions.

»   *How many year groups are there in Key Stage 1?*

»   *Why are there more year groups in Key Stage 2? Does this change your expectations for long- or mid-term planning?*

»   *Choose one of the core subject areas. What are the main differences in the content across the two key stages?*

Although as a primary specialist you are expected to know and understand the range of subject areas, it is important to concentrate on the core subjects as they underpin much of the learning across the curriculum. The following sections deal with the teaching of English, mathematics and science: the information here is not sufficient on its own and you will need to undertake wider reading of relevant subject-specific texts. However, it does provide a starting point for reflecting on the planning and teaching of each core area.

Teaching English

The ability to communicate in spoken and written English underpins learning across the curriculum and is a life skill. Much of the curriculum relies upon pupils making sense of texts, be they fiction or non-fiction, written or multi-media, dramatised or recited, and equally much assessment is based on the pupils' ability to construct texts appropriately. Teaching English, whether discretely or through a cross-curricular approach, is a key part of a primary teacher's day. By the time you qualify, your own subject knowledge should be secure and you will need a sound understanding of things that might be new to you such as systematic synthetic phonics.

The current primary English programme of study (DfE, 2013b) is separated into three areas, and while these areas develop concurrently throughout the curriculum it is helpful to consider the order of acquisition and interaction between them.

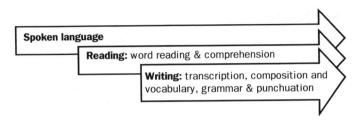

Figure 7.2 *Elements of the primary English programme of study.*

Critical questions

» *In the model above it is assumed that spoken language will be a part of the pupil's experience before reading and writing. Do you agree? Can you think of a better model to represent the English curriculum?*

» *Think back to how you learned to communicate in your first language. Did you learn these elements separately or together? For example, can you remember being taught to write and was it linked to being able to read or discuss?*

» *Standard English, language structure and language variation are themes that run through the English programme of study. Are there differences in spoken and written standard English? Do you model standard English in your own speech and writing? If not, how can you address this?*

CASE STUDY

Hannah's past experience: overcoming negative preconceptions

In a pre-practice tutorial Hannah, a trainee, admits her concerns about teaching English as a 'boring' subject.

I didn't enjoy English at school, especially leading up to GCSE. I always preferred more practical subjects like PE. I know I have to teach literacy in school, but I have to admit I am more interested in teaching other areas of the curriculum. Luckily my school timetables the boring things like grammar and writing in the morning so the afternoon is free for the fun stuff.

Comment on Hannah's story

In this case Hannah is in danger of transferring her negative perception of the subject to her pupils. Due to her own experiences she is unable to see the teaching of literacy skills as something that can be fun and engaging for pupils. This can be a serious issue in any area of the curriculum; it is important that all teaching is approached in a positive and knowledgeable way in order to ensure your pupils receive the best possible learning experience.

Critical questions

»   *How do you feel about teaching the English curriculum? Is your view affected by your own learning in school?*

»   *Does all learning have to be 'fun' to be engaging and worthwhile? Think of learning outside of the classroom, for example learning to drive or learning to cook: is every task 'fun'?*

»   *Reflect on Hannah's use of the word 'boring': how might this belief affect her practice?*

Secure subject knowledge is a key element of successful literacy teaching. It is very important to address gaps in your own understanding in order to ensure you are planning appropriately challenging lessons. It can be helpful to identify your areas of strength and areas for development for the different parts of the programme of study, although it is not intended that they be taught in isolation.

Teaching spoken language

Spoken language for years 1–6 within the national curriculum (DfE 2013b) is found at the beginning of the programme of study rather than embedded in the year group/age phase sections, but it is still a statutory requirement across the primary age range. There are 12 bullet points which detail what pupils should be taught, and it will be up to you as the teacher to embed these into your planning. Each of the bullet points applies to all of the age groups and phases: your subject knowledge and understanding of language acquisition and development will need to be secure enough to plan appropriately for the age of the pupils.

It might seem obvious, but it is important to remember that speaking and listening are not the same thing. They are complementary processes but often not distinguishable from each other in school-based learning, and in assessment in particular. Teachers utilise pupils' listening skills during lessons; discussion and oral presentation are frequently present on lesson plans across a range of subject areas; however, the explicit teaching of listening skills alongside the development of effective oral communication is a common feature of the most successful schools, though not always evident in all classroom environments.

Extended thinking

»   *Using Figure 7.3, try to identify which statement from the programme of study relates to each aspect of spoken language: two have been given as an example. Do all the statements fit neatly into the categories identified? What new or different categories might be needed?*

»   *What lesson activities have you seen that would allow pupils to develop these skills? Have they involved explicit teaching of spoken language or have pupils been expected to use the skills without any guidance?*

Teaching reading

The teaching of reading has long been a contested area, with many models for effective learning being put forward that often appear to be contradictory. After the Independent Review of the

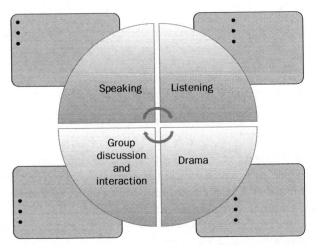

Figure 7.3 *The key skills, knowledge and understanding unique to each strand of spoken language.*

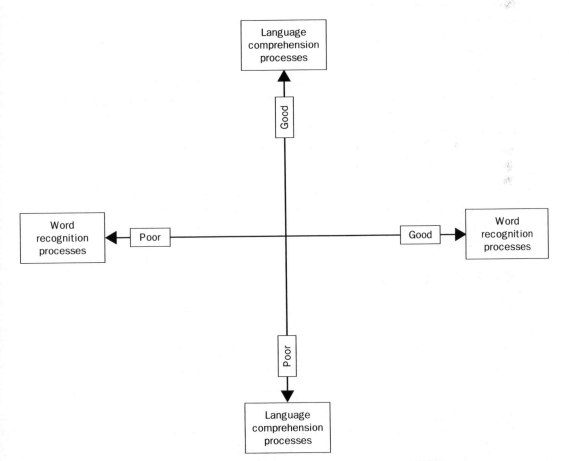

Figure 7.4 *The Simple View of Reading, based on Gough and Tunmer (1986).*

Teaching of Early Reading (DfES, 2006) was published, much of the focus switched to a model based on earlier work by Gough and Tunmer (1986) called the Simple View of Reading (SVoR) (see Figure 7.4). This defines the reading process as consisting of two distinct elements:

- Word recognition processes: these are time limited; it is expected that children will have acquired the necessary skills for reading and spelling words by the end of Key Stage 1.

- Language (linguistic) comprehension processes: these continue to develop throughout children's education and beyond.

The prime approach recommended for teaching reading is systematic synthetic phonics, which enables word recognition; and guided reading is key in developing language comprehension. In 2012/13 the government introduced a phonics screening check in Key Stage 1 and a new Key Stage 2 English grammar, punctuation and spelling test. Information regarding both of these tests and other assessment arrangements can be found at http://www.education.gov.uk/schools/teachingandlearning/assessment.

Systematic synthetic phonics (SSP)

Systematic synthetic phonics (SSP) is an approach that relies on readers and spellers understanding how the sounds in words (phonemes) correspond to the way they are written or represented on the page (graphemes). This grapheme/phoneme correspondence (GPC) is synthesised (hence synthetic) in order to allow readers to blend sounds together to read words, or segment the sounds to identify the most likely spelling.

However, the complex alphabetic code used by written English means this process is not straightforward. The 26 letters of the alphabet can be used to represent 44 different sounds in spoken English, with 144 single-letter or letter-combination graphemes; many phonemes can be represented by more than one grapheme, and many graphemes can be used to represent more than one phoneme, for example the graphemes 'th' and 'ough' sound different in the words though and thought.

There are many published schemes which provide lesson plans and guidance on SSP, but the key is to develop your own subject knowledge and understanding through observations of teachers and wider reading. Helpful guidance is provided in the national curriculum (DfE, 2013b) English Appendix 1: Spelling.

Critical questions

»   *How many of the 44 phonemes in English can you identify? How many are vowel sounds and how many are consonant sounds?*

»   *SSP uses technical terms which can be intimidating for trainees. Find the meaning of the following words and begin your own phonics glossary:*

blending	
segmenting	
digraph	
trigraph	
CVC	

» Are there any other terms you have read in relation to synthetic phonics which can be added to this list?

» Not all readers progress at the same rate. How can a knowledge and understanding of SSP help you teach children in Key Stage 2?

Other reading strategies

CASE STUDY

Paola's reading query

During my training a lot of time has been given to learning about synthetic phonics: I have observed teachers, planned lessons and taught them in school. Then on my last placement I was invited to a moderation meeting where staff discussed children's ability to use a range of reading strategies. I realised I didn't know what the other strategies were or when I am supposed to teach them! If phonics is about word recognition then what strategies are used to teach about comprehension?

Comment on Paola's story

Paola has identified that reading is about more than word recognition but is not sure how to address this. An effective way she could teach children the skills, knowledge and understanding needed to comprehend what they are reading is through guided reading.

Guided reading is a short, focused session which allows the teacher to plan a specific learning objective related to reading. Like the teaching of systematic synthetic phonics, it has a structured teaching sequence (see Figure 7.5).

A comprehensive description of what each element consists of can be found in Teaching English, Language and Literacy by Wyse et al., (2013) pages 180–82 (see Taking it further at the end of this chapter for details).

This does not deal with the question of what reading strategies are available for fluent readers to use when trying to comprehend a text.

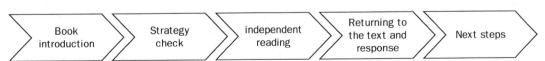

Figure 7.5 Guided reading.

Critical questions

»   *Think about how you are making sense of this chapter: what different mental processes are you using?*

»   *What sort of prior knowledge is needed before you can understand a text like this one?*

»   *Are the skills you are using transferable to different genres?*

There are at least nine strategies that effective readers use to comprehend a text:

1.   close reading;

2.   skimming;

3.   scanning;

4.   inferring;

5.   predicting;

6.   questioning;

7.   empathising;

8.   visualising;

9.   reading backwards and forwards.

It is important that you understand what each strategy for reading entails so you can model it for pupils. There are physical and mental differences between skim reading and scanning, for example: you need to consider the implications and appropriate uses for each in order to effectively teach the skills. Other strategies and models also exist, so make sure you read around this area of the curriculum so that you feel confident that you can address any problems children may have in acquiring the skills needed to access texts.

Teaching writing

The writing process is made up of two elements:

•   **Composition** is about the content: who am I writing for/who will read this? What do I want to tell the reader? What is the genre?

•   **Transcription** deals with the mechanics of writing: how am I going to present my writing? It is the aspect that covers legible handwriting, accurate spelling and use of punctuation.

English Appendix 2: Vocabulary, grammar and punctuation in the national curriculum (DfE, 2013b) provides some guidance on when and what aspects should be introduced, along with a glossary to help develop your understanding of metalanguage.

Using a framework such as that suggested in Talk for Writing (National Strategies, 2008) allows you to plan a sequence of lessons all leading to independent writing of a particular genre. It does rely on transcription skills being taught concurrently (see the section above on SSP for opportunities to practise letter formation, for example); and on extensive subject knowledge of the key features of different genres and non-fiction text types.

Critical questions

» *How many different fiction genres are you familiar with? What are the key features of each?*

» *What are the non-fiction text types?*

» *Do you think knowledge and understanding of composition is more valuable than transcription skills? Do you think they are equal? Or should transcription be addressed before composition? Try to identify your own values and beliefs regarding writing: what is the potential impact on your assessment of pupils' progress?*

Checklist for English planning, teaching and assessment

It is useful to think of the process of teaching English in terms of three elements: planning, teaching and assessment. The following literacy checklist can be used to evaluate your practice in all three areas to ensure you are addressing the key issues, either as self-reflection or as part of a planned observation or discussion with your school mentor.

Planning

- Are learning objectives clear and visible? Have you planned an opportunity to share these with pupils?

- Is the lesson linked to prior learning in a purposeful way?

- Is the planned teaching sequence appropriate for the area of literacy being taught?

  - Is high-quality SSP planned using a clear revise → teach → practice →apply format?

  - Does guided reading include a strategy check/independent reading/return to the text and response? Is the chosen text appropriate for the level of independent reading?

- Has the deployment of adult support been effectively planned for? (See Chapter 4 for guidance on working with support staff.)

- Is there evidence of planned differentiation, including challenge for more able pupils and personalised learning, where applicable?

Teaching

- Is the introduction focused and engaging?

- Is there a recap of relevant strategies that will support the intended new learning?

- Are the children made aware of audience and purpose, both when studying text types in reading or writing their own texts?

- Do you use a range of interactive and multi-sensory teaching strategies?

  - Is there evidence of teacher modelling or scribing when doing shared activities?

  - Do children read and write independently rather than reading aloud to each other or writing together in guided tasks?

- Do you encourage children to apply learned phonic skills (segmenting and blending) to read and spell words outside of phonics sessions?

- Do you use appropriate technical vocabulary, for example when teaching grammar?

- Is appropriate subject knowledge evident in your teaching?

- Is En1 embedded in the lesson and are children appropriately scaffolded where necessary?

- Is there evidence of appropriate challenge and differentiation at the point of learning?

- Is intervention appropriate and at the point of need?

Assessment

- Has assessment been clearly linked to the teaching objectives through appropriate success criteria for spoken language, reading and writing?

- Is formative assessment visible through observation, monitoring and questioning?

  - Is feedback appropriate and provided in a timely manner?

- Has formative observation and assessment of the application of skills, for example phonics, been recorded alongside data collected from the marking of writing?

  - Is assessment data used to inform the planning of next steps?

Teaching mathematics

Mathematics (often called numeracy in primary schools) is an area of the curriculum that many find difficult, with issues of confidence and competence, so as a trainee teacher it is your responsibility to address any areas of weakness in your own understanding. Wider reading of theoretical subject-based and curriculum support materials is a necessary part of this and should be done prior to and during any planning to ensure you are adequately prepared for teaching the content of your lesson.

Mathematics is a subject with a wide array of potential applications and in relation to the current curriculum (DfE, 2013b) it is important that fluency, mathematical reasoning and problem solving is at the heart of your mathematics teaching. However, when referring to the national curriculum (ibid), you will notice there is no specific section entitled mathematical reasoning and problem solving. Rather, it is assumed that you will draw upon the interconnected nature of mathematics from the distinct programmes of study to inform your teaching and to embed problem solving, mathematical reasoning and fluency into the children's experience of learning. There is an expectation that your pupils should make *rich connections* across mathematical concepts in order to competently solve increasingly *sophisticated problems* and apply this to science and other subjects (DfE, 2013b).

Critical questions

The current programmes of study for primary mathematics (DfE, 2013b) are divided into four distinct fields. Look at Figure 7.6. Each diagram represents a different way of looking at the national curriculum for mathematics.

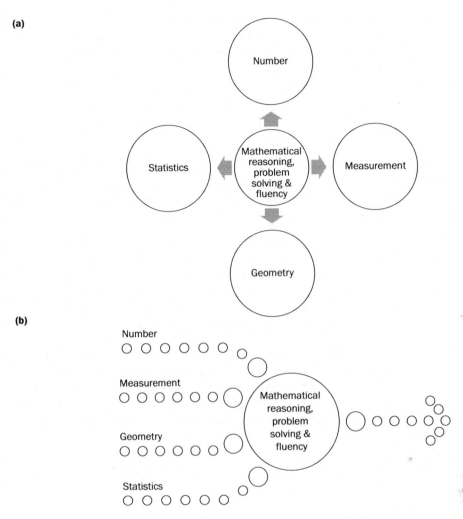

Figure 7.6 *Ways of looking at the national curriculum for mathematics.*

» *What are the implications of using each approach for planning and teaching?*

» *Which model is preferable for appropriate teaching and learning in the primary classroom? Explain your answer.*

» *Which one reflects the process as you have observed it in school?*

» *Which approach is advocated by the primary mathematics curriculum?*

While the first model implies that mathematical reasoning, problem solving and fluency is the starting point for planning, it is often the case that teachers who lack confidence in teaching mathematics see it as the end result of the learning. This can lead pupils to find the process confusing and without purpose, and it is vital that you think systematically about the practical applications of the maths being taught, alongside the process, to ensure you address such issues. Furthermore you should ensure that you plan for pupil talk within your mathematics lessons in order to develop pupils' mathematical vocabulary and their ability to justify, argue or prove.

Within a school the mathematics documentation is sometimes referred to as a calculation policy, and it is used to detail the progression in skills, knowledge and understanding across the operations of addition, subtraction, multiplication and division alongside current teaching strategies and methods. The calculation policy will help you understand what the school subject co-ordinator for numeracy expects to see in your lessons, so it is important that you obtain a copy and read it. The mathematics curriculum also provides examples of formal written methods for addition, subtraction, multiplication and division although this is not an exhaustive list.

Many schools use published schemes which you may be asked to utilise. These provide a useful framework, often accompanied by specific resources, but it is still important that you understand how to facilitate the learning for your pupils and also how it links to the national curriculum programme of study (DfE, 2013b).

Even if your school setting is using a prescriptive scheme, it is possible for you to demonstrate your understanding through annotations and reflective responses. You can attach articles and useful subject knowledge texts to your planning which demonstrates how you are engaging with the underpinning theories and pedagogies; you can note alternative resources or strategies for future practice; you can link the mathematical concepts to other curriculum lessons in order to show how you are enabling pupils to apply their learning in mathematics.

If there is no scheme provided it is important that you consider the mathematical process and progression in skills. Where are your pupils in their learning across the different attainment targets? How do you know? This is a good place to start when planning any curriculum lesson, but particularly relevant when teaching systematic mathematical concepts. Lessons can then be planned as a series rather than one-off experiences, allowing children to build on prior learning in a meaningful way.

Checklist for mathematics planning, teaching and assessment

The following mathematics checklist can be used to evaluate your practice in planning, teaching and assessment to ensure you are addressing the key issues, either as self-reflection or as part of a planned observation or discussion with your school mentor.

Planning

*   Are learning objectives clear and visible? Have you planned the opportunity to share these with pupils?

*   Is pupil engagement enabled through flexible teaching approaches?

*   Is the learning systematic and does it build upon prior learning?

    –   Does mental work provide an opportunity to practise skills that have already been taught?

    –   Is there further opportunity for the recap and review of transferable skills?

*   Has the deployment of adult support been effectively planned for? (See Chapter 4 for guidance on working with support staff.)

- Is there evidence of planned differentiation, including challenge for more able pupils and personalised learning, where applicable?

Teaching

- Is there evidence of new learning as well as recap and review of previously taught mathematics?
- Is the learning interactive and multi-sensory?
- Is the process of 'doing the process' appropriately modelled by the teacher?
- Are there opportunities for pupils to choose appropriate mathematics to tackle problem solving?
  - Are they taught to present results in an appropriate and organised way?
- Is there the opportunity for the use of mathematical language to communicate ideas?
  - Do they provide reasons for their mathematical decisions?
- Is there evidence of appropriate challenge and differentiation at the point of learning?
- Is intervention appropriate and at the point of need?

Assessment

- Has assessment been clearly linked to the teaching objectives through appropriate success criteria?
- Is this visible throughout the planning and teaching elements of the lesson?
- Is formative assessment visible through observation, monitoring and questioning?
  - Is feedback appropriate and provided in a timely manner?
- Is assessment data recorded in order to inform the planning of next steps?

Teaching science

At the heart of the current primary science curriculum (DfE, 2013b) is *working scientifically*; it is about discovering how science works using a hands-on investigative approach. When teaching children about science you are also encouraged to enable pupils to experience and observe phenomena linked to the statutory programmes of study which are organised for each year group that a child will progress through in their primary school career. These statutory programmes are organised into discrete topics which indicate the substantive science context to be covered by the end of Year 6.

CASE STUDY

Keiran's experience

I felt quite confident about teaching science as I enjoyed it at school. During my teaching practice my mentor asked me to plan a KS2 lesson on living things and their habitats. I had been at the school for about two weeks already but I realised I hadn't seen science as it was taught during my PPA (planning, preparation and assessment) time and I never thought to go and watch the lessons; I'd been getting really good feedback for my planning and teaching up to this point and I didn't want to wreck my profile by asking for too much help. I found a lesson plan on the internet which had clear Sc1 objectives and even provided extension worksheets.

After I taught the lesson the teacher gave me feedback, which was all right but she said she had to grade me quite low for subject knowledge because I hadn't actually done any enquiry activities with the children. I was devastated! It wasn't on the plan, so I didn't realise I was supposed to include it.

Critical questions

»   When looking at living things and their habitats, what sort of investigations linked to 'working scientifically' could be planned that enable children to develop skills of enquiry?

»   How could Keiran have ensured that the children were moving beyond classroom- and computer-based research?

Comment on Keiran's story

As demonstrated in Keiran's case, the structure of the curriculum, allied to a focus on *working scientifically*, can sometimes lead to confusion. Sometimes *working scientifically* is planned as an addition rather than an integral part of childrens' learning; in Keiran's experience it was not made explicit on the published plan and consequently left out of the lesson entirely. It is important to recognise that, under curriculum requirements, children must use a mixture of classroom-based research and activities with *working scientifically* integrated into pupils' study in order to develop their scientific knowledge and understanding. Thus it might be beneficial to visualise *working scientifically* as encompassing all other areas of study rather than as a separate entity only to be planned for using discrete activities.

In the Ofsted report *Successful Science* (2011d) it was recognised that subject knowledge and staff expertise was a pivotal factor in challenging able pupils. Read the extracts from the report below and think about the implications for pupils' learning.

Although pupils' progress in science was good or outstanding in 70% of the primary schools visited, a lack of specialist expertise limited the challenge for some more able pupils. (page 6)

Despite some positive initiatives, such as the Primary Science Quality Mark and the Association for Science Education's publication for primary schools 'Be safe', there has been insufficient professional development in science to tackle the lack of confidence among primary teachers, particularly in their understanding of scientific enquiry skills and the physical sciences. (page 7)

Extended thinking

» How can these implications be addressed? List the strategies for developing subject specialist expertise and understanding of scientific enquiry skills in science.

» What are the key terms needed to teach scientific enquiry? Develop a glossary of the technical scientific vocabulary you would like to embed into your practice.

Checklist for science planning, teaching and assessment

The following science checklist can be used to evaluate your practice in planning, teaching and assessment, either as self-reflection or as part of a planned observation or discussion with your school mentor.

Planning

- Are learning objectives linked to the programmes of study clear and visible? Have you planned the opportunity to share these with pupils?
- Is there a clear focus on *working scientifically?*
- Is the learning systematic and does it build upon prior learning?
  - Is it part of a cohesive unit of work?
  - Is the lesson appropriate for the stage of learning?
- Has the deployment of adult support been effectively planned for? (See Chapter 4 for guidance on working with support staff.)
- *Is there evidence of planned differentiation, including challenge for more able pupils and personalised learning, where applicable?*

Teaching

- Is the learning interactive and multi-sensory?
- Is the process of planning a fair test appropriately modelled by the teacher?
- Are there opportunities for pupils to choose appropriate methods to obtain evidence?
- Are they taught to present results in an appropriate and organised way?
- Is there opportunity for the use of oral and written language to communicate ideas?
  - Is there opportunity to make comparisons and draw conclusions?
  - Do they provide reasons for their scientific decisions?
- Is there evidence of appropriate challenge and differentiation at the point of learning?
- Is intervention appropriate and at the point of need?

Assessment

- Has assessment been clearly linked to the teaching objectives through appropriate success criteria?
- Is this visible throughout the planning and teaching elements of the lesson?
- Is formative assessment visible through observation, monitoring and questioning?
  - Is feedback appropriate and provided in a timely manner?
  - Does it include reference to the enquiry skills identified in the plan?
- Is assessment data recorded in order to inform the planning of next steps?

Chapter reflections

Teaching any subject should be based on your underpinning values and beliefs about effective learning: it shouldn't matter whether it is a traditionally academic subject or a more practical area of the curriculum, all your planned lessons should be engaging, purposeful and underpinned by subject knowledge. However, particular skills, knowledge and understanding in the core subjects are essential for pupils if they are to access learning across the curriculum, so it is vital you feel confident in helping to develop these.

Critical points

» *Use the curriculum and/or subject frameworks as a starting point for planning rather than as an end checklist.*

» *Ensure you link planning, teaching and assessment of learning.*

» *Think about the intended learning and match this to appropriate activities and strategies.*

» *Take risks: be adventurous in your teaching, even in areas of the curriculum perceived to be mundane. For example, grammar doesn't have to be boring!*

Taking it further

Allen, M (2010) *Misconceptions in Primary Science*. Maidenhead: OUP.

Barmby, P and Bolden, D (2014) *Understanding and Enriching Problem Solving in Primary Mathematics*. Northwich: Critical Publishing.

Boaler, J (2010) *The Elephant in the Classroom: Helping Children Learn and Love Maths*. London: Souvenir Press.

Briggs, M (2013) *Teaching and Learning Early Years Mathematics: Subject and Pedagogic Knowledge*. Northwich: Critical Publishing.

Cooke, V and Howard, C (2014) *Practical Ideas for Teaching Primary Science*. Northwich: Critical Publishing.

Cremin, T (2009) *Teaching English Creatively*. London: Routledge.

Cross, A and Bowden, A (2010) *Essential Primary Science*. Maidenhead: OUP.

Glazzard, J and Stokoe, J (2013) *Teaching Systematic Synthetic Phonics and Early English*. Northwich: Critical Publishing.

Haylock, D (2010) (4th edn) *Mathematics Explained for Primary Teachers*. London: Sage.

Horton, S and Bingle, B (2014) *Lessons in Teaching Grammar in Primary Schools*. London: Learning Matters.

Joliffe, W and Waugh, D with Carss, A (2012) *Teaching Systematic Synthetic Phonics in Primary Schools*. London: Routledge.

Johnston, R and Watson, J (2007) *Teaching Synthetic Phonics*. Exeter: Learning Matters.

Montague-Smith, A and Price, A J (2012) (3rd edn) *Mathematics in Early Years Education*. London: Routledge.

Pound, L and Lee, T (2011) *Teaching Mathematics Creatively*. London: Routledge.

Waugh, D and Neaum, S (2013) *Beyond Early Reading*. Northwich: Critical Publishing.

Wenham, M (2007) *200 Science Investigations for Young Students*. London: Paul Chapman Publications.

Wenham, M and Ovens, P (2010) (3rd edn) *Understanding Primary Science*. London: Sage Publications.

Whetton, C, (2009) A Brief History of a Testing Time: National Curriculum Assessment in England 1989–2008. *Educational Research*, 51: 2, 137–59.

Wyse, D, Jones, R, Bradford, H and Wolpert, M A (2013) (3rd edn) *Teaching English, Language and Literacy*. Abingdon: Routledge.

8 Teaching inclusively

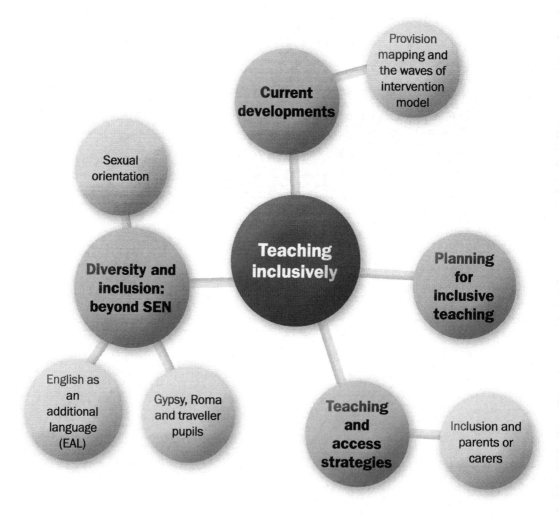

Current developments

Provision mapping and the waves of intervention model

Sexual orientation

Diversity and inclusion: beyond SEN

Teaching inclusively

Planning for inclusive teaching

English as an additional language (EAL)

Gypsy, Roma and traveller pupils

Teaching and access strategies

Inclusion and parents or carers

Teachers' Standards (DfE, 2011c)

1 Set high expectations which inspire, motivate and challenge pupils

- set goals that stretch and challenge pupils of all backgrounds, abilities and dispositions.

5 Adapt teaching to respond to the strengths and needs of all pupils

- know when and how to differentiate appropriately, using approaches which enable pupils to be taught effectively

- have a secure understanding of how a range of factors can inhibit pupils' ability to learn, and how best to overcome these

- demonstrate an awareness of the physical, social and intellectual development of children, and know how to adapt teaching to support pupils' education at different stages of development

- have a clear understanding of the needs of all pupils, including those with special educational needs, those of high ability, those with English as an additional language, those with disabilities, and be able to use and evaluate distinctive teaching approaches to engage and support them.

Introduction

Inclusive teaching in the UK is intended to ensure that learning is accessible and appropriately challenging for all pupils, regardless of circumstance. Among a myriad of other issues, it includes:

- planning for specific learning difficulties;

- gender, ethnicity, cultural and spiritual factors;

- permanent disabilities;

- short-term or temporary barriers to learning.

It is based on the principle of equality of opportunity for all, and thus the focus is on what provision is available for those groups who might otherwise be excluded from mainstream education. As a trainee teacher you have the same responsibilities for effective and inclusive teaching as your mentor in school.

Current developments

Since the launch of the DfE (2011a) SEN green paper Support and Aspiration: A New Approach to Special Educational Needs and Disability in 2011, education has been undergoing what the DfE calls *the biggest programme of reform in the education and health support for children with special educational needs (SEN) and disabilities in 30 years* (DfE, 2012a). The introduction of legislation detailing provision for children and young people with SEN (updated in January 2015) provided a coherent statutory framework, intended to streamline the assessment process and draw together education and healthcare services. This was designed to provide a single statutory 0–25 assessment process.

The *SEND Code of Practice: 0 to 25 Years* (DfE, 2015a) 'provides statutory guidance on duties, policies and procedures relating to Part 3 of the Children and Families Act 2014 and associated regulations and applies to England.' Guidance for supporting the needs of pupils with mild to moderate SEN include a simple school-based category to help teachers focus on raising attainment. It also gives parents or young people the right to a personal budget for their support, alongside the Local Offer, which will address how local authorities are planning provision for these groups of children and young people. The code of practice makes it a requirement that schools and local authorities must work together to review and establish the Local Offer. The intention is to require local authorities and health services to work in partnership to plan and commission the services that children, young people and families need.

It is useful to understand the roles and responsibilities held by different stakeholders in the local context. The Code includes a table which details Local Accountability, and the section that refers to schools is as follows:

Table 8.1

Agency	Key responsibilities for SEN or Disability	Accountability
Maintained nurseries and schools (including academies)	Mainstream schools have duties to use best endeavours to make the provision required to meet the SEN of children and young people. All schools must publish details of what SEN provision is available through the information report and co-operate with the local authority in drawing up and reviewing the Local Offer. Schools also have duties to make reasonable adjustments for disabled children and young people, to support medical conditions and to inform parents and young people if SEN provision is made for them. More information about the role of early years settings, schools and post-16 institutions is given in Chapters 5 to 7.	Accountability is through Ofsted and the annual report that schools have to provide to parents on their children's progress.

Taken from the Local Accountability summary table, SEND Code of Practice(DfE, 2015a, pp. 56–8)

However it is important that you familiarise yourself with all the different bodies involved in joint commissioning of services in order to fully support pupils with SEND, particularly as individual education, health and care (EHC) plans are meant to inform Joint Strategic Needs Assessment (JSNA) within local authorities.

For more information on what is meant by the Local Offer, the Council for Disabled Children has provided briefing notes which can be found at http://www.councilfordisabledchildren. org.uk/media/246954/local%20offer.pdf.

Although these changes have affected practice in school since September 2014 it will take time for them to embed, and you may still see evidence of provision mapping and individual education plans (IEPs) while on placement. High Quality Teaching as the first wave of intervention is still enshrined in the current code. Therefore it is useful to know a bit about these and the three waves of teaching and intervention.

Provision mapping and the waves of intervention model

Provision mapping is an approach to planning which encompasses all the different strategies that will enable pupils' needs to be met within and beyond the school context. It is linked to whole school initiatives introduced during the implementation of the National Strategies (2005–2010); Guidance highlighted six key areas for school leaders to consider (DfE, 2012b):

1. Knowing the vulnerabilities of all pupils;

2. Developing the workforce;

3. Developing the quality of provision;

4. Identifying the right provision for all pupils;

5. Monitoring and evaluating impact and analysing the data;

6. Assessment and tracking.

Although the key areas were designed for school leaders, they provide a helpful starting point for reflection on your own practice.

Critical questions

» *Think about a class you have taught or are currently teaching: what information can you provide about at least three individual pupils against each of the headings? For example, for 'Developing the workforce' did any of the pupils require staff to receive particular professional development?*

» *Which areas do you feel less confident about in your knowledge of provision? How might you develop your understanding of those areas?*

» *What is the difference between 'Monitoring and evaluating impact' and 'Assessment and tracking'? They deal with different aspects of provision mapping, but are you clear on the distinctions between the two areas?*

Provision mapping is often accompanied by the three waves of inclusion model (see Figure 8.1), which details how a particular setting can identify and address educational needs. Each wave specifies the teaching and learning entitlement for pupils.

It is important that waves 2 and 3 do not become confused with the terms School Action (SA) and School Action Plus (SA+), terms that are linked to statements of SEN and are not interchangeable with provision mapping, which encompasses all pupils. The implementation of the single assessment process in 2014 was designed to address this confusion. In your setting the school SENCO will be able to explain how learning needs and overcoming barriers are addressed, so seek them out to help you understand the process in practice!

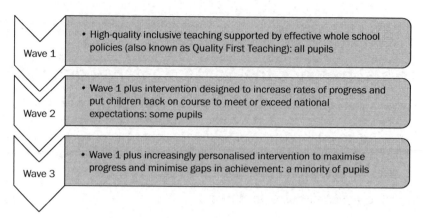

Figure 8.1 *The three waves of inclusion, based on a model developed by the National Strategies.*

Planning for inclusive teaching

As a result of developing your knowledge of the historical and current context of SEN and inclusive teaching it might be dawning on you that planning for differentiation and adapting your teaching to support pupils' education actually requires a significant understanding of the range of barriers to learning, alongside a secure knowledge of a range of teaching strategies for use across the curriculum. It is also vital to get to know your pupils' needs in depth through appropriate use of data.

CASE STUDY

Hayley's 'inclusive' lesson

I collected a lot of information about the children in my class at the beginning of my placement. One of the pupils, Chloe, had learning difficulties and the teacher said that meant I had to identify her on every lesson plan and make special provision for her. She had a TA who worked with her so generally that is what I put on my plan.

During a formal observation of an art lesson my tutor asked me about Chloe's difficulties: what were her targets, how did I make sure she was planned for appropriately. I pointed to the bit on my lesson plan to show I had the TA working with her. In the feedback afterwards my tutor pointed out that Chloe had difficulties with literacy and that none of her targets indicated she needed extra TA support in art beyond accessing any instructions written on the board. In fact, she was becoming so dependent on the TA in my lessons that she hadn't even sorted out the materials she needed for herself, preferring to wait until the TA told her what to do or did it for her.

Critical questions

» What advice would you give Hayley with regard to supporting Chloe appropriately in lessons other than literacy?

» Are there alternative ways, other than working with a TA, to support her when literacy skills are required?

Comment on Hayley's lesson

In Hayley's case she misunderstood the nature of Chloe's needs, and this led to an over-reliance on TA support across the curriculum by both Chloe and Hayley. For more practical activities Hayley needed to identify 'tasks' for the TA (with her agreement) which took her away from one-to-one support at points in the lesson when literacy support was not required; this would in turn mean that Chloe had to start working more independently in practical activities. However, there are other inclusive strategies, such as visual timetables or desktop prompts, which might support Chloe more effectively than a continued reliance on adult support.

In order to plan for Quality First teaching to address individual needs it is useful to refer to the following conceptual model.

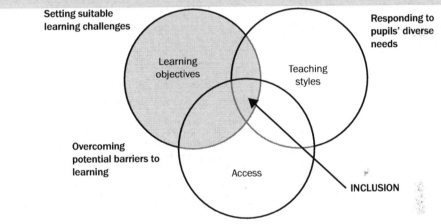

Figure 8.2 *Circles of inclusion, based on a model developed by the National Strategies, DfE.*

Effective inclusive planning can be embedded into a teacher's usual planning format, so you can adapt whatever your training provider or placement setting have given you as a frame for planning. Draw on the three principles highlighted on the circles of inclusion (see Figure 8.2): for each aspect of the lesson, and try to incorporate personal targets wherever possible or necessary. As in Chloe's case, having a particular need may not affect every learning activity, so it is important for you to consider each need and each activity in isolation when trying to determine what scaffolding or support might be required. Clearly set out the role of any additional adults who will be working in the lesson, and think about the experience and expertise of all adults, including yourself, when planning how to deploy staff (see Chapter 4). In the most effective provision, planning is collaborative, so don't be afraid to seek advice from staff with extensive experience or specialist training.

One aspect of effective pedagogy not to be overlooked is the involvement of the pupil. Support will be more meaningful if it is worked out with the pupil/s involved rather than imposed on them. In the 2015 NCTL research report *What makes great pedagogy and great professional development* one of the key messages was the importance of talking with, listening to and involving pupils in helping shape their experience. The research findings have led to the claim that "Effective pedagogies give serious consideration to pupil voice" (NCTL, 2015); a case study example identifies intervention designed using pupil input as evidence of this in practice. In Chloe's case she could be involved in developing, trialling and piloting support materials, giving feedback on what works for her and what doesn't, rather than having strategies 'done to' her.

Critical question

» Use an expanded copy of the chart below to think about how the following special educational needs and disabilities (SEND) could affect classroom practice. What teaching strategies could be used to enable learning to take place?

- ADD/ADHD/behaviour difficulties
- Attachment difficulties/disorders
- Autism and Asperger's
- Dyscalculia
- Dyslexia
- Dyspraxia

- Epilepsy
- Foetal alcohol syndrome
- Fragile X
- Physical disability
- Prader-Willi syndrome
- Visual/hearing impairments

SEND	What are the likely barriers to learning?	Impact on classroom: potential issues	Possible strategies: teaching/access

The suggestions in the Taking it further section of this chapter will help you complete this task if you are unsure of the definitions for the conditions listed.

Teaching and access strategies

Some teaching strategies you might want to consider incorporating in your practice include the following:

- Multi-sensory – try to plan for learning that uses more than one style of activity; this links to:

- Visual and tangible aids – for example story sacks, real objects, signs/symbols, photographs, different number lines, computer animations, visual timetables, magnetic boards ... (the list is as long as your creative imagination!);

- Interactive (active pupil involvement) – holding up cards, writing on individual whiteboards, coming to the front to take a role, other drama activities such as conscience alley or forum theatre;

- Tasks simplified/extended – differentiated as appropriate;

- Group/paired/individual activities – think about offering a variety of groupings for the same activity: some children might prefer to work alone, others in a group;

- Alternative ways of responding – sorting and labelling, ready-made text, scribing, recording oral responses, charts and diagrams;

In addition, consider how you are utilising access strategies within the lesson itself.

- Check all pupils can see/hear you no matter where they are sitting (this is particularly important in classrooms where tables are grouped or there are obstacles such as pillars).

- When introducing new vocabulary display it on noticeboards or 'washing lines'; ensure difficult vocabulary is clarified, displayed and revisited to remind pupils of the meaning and the spelling.

- Find ways to check pupils have understood instructions, for example 'explain what you have to do in your own words' or 'tell the person next to you the first thing they have to do now'.

- Provide thinking and processing time when asking for a response: a simple way is to establish the convention of not allowing hands-up until you as the questioner have counted to five (silently is best to avoid disrupting the thinking) and then indicated you are ready for answers. Suddenly the whole class has a chance to respond rather than the same quick thinkers!

- Model the expected process: as the subject expert, the children look to you to see how it should be done, and unless it is a formal assessment activity there is no reason why you can't show them. Lift the lid on your thinking as you do it to make your decision-making process explicit.

- Make time and expectations clear through sharing objectives and giving time-checks during independent learning.

- Provide resources to help pupils work independently, such as left-handed equipment, large-print versions of text or oral instructions left on a recording device.

These are by no means exhaustive lists of the teaching and access strategies available to you, so do use your PPA time in school to observe the good practice around you and add to your resource bank of ideas.

Inclusion and parents or carers

The Ofsted report Schools and Parents (2011c) identified that good home–school links *helped to narrow gaps between the attainment of underachieving pupils and their peers*. This was true for those with SEND, EAL and in a range of social or cultural situations. While it might seem obvious that this link between parents and teachers would be beneficial, it is often difficult during a placement to see how you can establish effective communication with parents and carers. Some ideas to aid contact are discussed in Chapter 4 of this book. Parents are often contacted only to discuss problems with their child or if there has been an incident, which can then make the relationship a very negative one. So it is important to remember that parents are often the experts on their children: they know their interests, dislikes, triggers for anxiety or challenging behaviour and can offer advice on strategies which

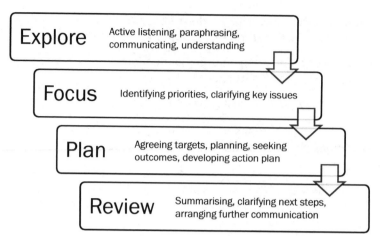

Figure 8.3 *Based on the model for the Structured Conversation (DCSF, 2009).*

are effective in supporting their child. They might be able to explain changes in behaviour as they will know if problems at home may have caused issues in the school environment.

The DfE (2011b) *Achievement for All National Evaluation: Final Report* found that the implementation of structured conversations with parents improved relationships dramatically, making it easier to take a holistic view of the child. Figure 8.3, provided for a structured conversation, might be useful if you do get the opportunity to speak with parents.

It is important to note that while most interactions between school and home will be with parents, you need to remember that some are cared for by others. Treat the contributions from carers as respectfully and sensitively as those from parents.

Diversity and inclusion: beyond SEN

There are other aspects to consider in an inclusive environment that do not involve special educational needs or disabilities. The wider perspective also includes social, racial, cultural and spiritual issues, English as an additional language (EAL), gender and sexual orientation. In order to start identifying the impact of this range of diversity, the remainder of the chapter presents a series of case studies as a starting point for your developing understanding.

Gypsy, Roma and traveller pupils

CASE STUDY

Bryan's story: traveller education

My placement school had a high number of traveller children on roll. I didn't know much about traveller communities other than what you sometimes see on TV, and to be honest much of that didn't seem very positive. During one lunchtime I spotted an incident in the playground: two boys were arguing, and suddenly started fighting. I helped the supervising staff separate the boys, who were sent to the head teacher. Later she said the fight had started because one of the boys was Roma, living on an official council traveller site and the other was an Irish traveller whose family had moved into the area temporarily: they had been carrying on an argument that had started between the two families outside of school. This was the first time I realised that there was more than one group of travellers! The head advised me to look at the county council's integrated services website, which gave me links to other information and resources; I realised I needed to read around the issues if I was going to understand how to teach these children effectively, as I have to admit I had written them off as argumentative and difficult to manage in the classroom.

I began to notice things around the school that indicated the staff were recognising and celebrating the children's home community: there was a book about counting in the reception classroom which had images from traveller communities and was in fact shaped like a caravan; the school had done an 'oral stories' project and invited parents to come in to talk about their childhood and the information was presented on a display board in the school hall with many stories from traveller parents; and there were posters around the school of celebrities and famous people that I subsequently learned came from traveller communities. When I had first entered the school I had no idea of the significance of all these things, but when I looked at it through the lens of someone who was a Roma or Irish traveller I realised how important it would be to them to feel their culture was valued.

Critical questions

» What barriers to learning might a pupil from a traveller community face?

» What do you know about Gypsy, Roma and traveller cultural values? How much of your understanding is based on solid, theoretical underpinning and how much is on perception?

» What other racial or ethnic groups may you need to consider in your placement setting? How can you ensure your classroom environment is welcoming and inclusive?

Comment on Bryan's story

Gypsy, Roma and traveller children were identified as the ethnic groups most 'at risk' educationally due to poor retention rates in school, and although this picture is improving (Wilkin et al., 2010) it is still an area of concern. Children from other cultures and ethnicities need to be included while not losing sight of the need to celebrate the culture of the majority: all pupils need a sense of belonging to the school community in order to feel accepted. A consistent focus on raising aspiration and celebrating diversity needs to be underpinned by a sympathetic understanding of the issues.

English as an additional language (EAL)

CASE STUDY

Kayleigh's problem: identifying learning needs with EAL children

The catchment area for my placement school included several foster families, so the school was experienced in working with them, their social workers and other members of integrated services to help support the children in school. One day a pupil, Karim, arrived who had been placed with a local foster family. Not only did he not speak English, no one even knew how old he was! The only information the foster parent could provide was that he was originally from a conflict area and had been smuggled across Europe; this is apparently classed as child-trafficking, which I hadn't realised before. On that first day I was asked to design a visual timetable for him using a software programme bought by the school. The school didn't have many EAL children, and certainly none with such little understanding of English, so certain issues arose during the day that also needed visual cues, for example a picture on the toilet door was met with a look of relief at break time!

The next day I was meant to teach a mathematics lesson about ordering and comparing fractions, and as I prepared the night before I suddenly realised I didn't know how to scaffold Karim's learning: I had no idea of his level of ability in maths! I had to think about what inclusive strategies and resources might make my lesson as practical and clear as possible; I also had to think about how I could make abstract concepts a bit more concrete. It made me realise that up until that point I had relied on being able to tell the children what to do and getting them to record their answers with pen and paper, which wasn't going to work for him.

Critical questions

» What parts of the mathematics lesson are likely to be most affected by Karim's language difficulties?

» Think back to the inclusive teaching and access strategies listed earlier in this chapter: which do you suggest that Kayleigh should try and why?

» How might Kayleigh start to identify any mathematical ability or address misunderstandings without Karim's ability to tell her?

Comment on Kayleigh's problem

It is important to try to avoid making assumptions regarding any pupil's capabilities, and in normal circumstances it would be advisable to speak to the parents of children with EAL, with the help of an interpreter if necessary, to try to establish the child's level of ability. In Karim's case he is not living with his parents, and his foster carer has very little extra information to provide; they may, however, have noticed things at home that might help, so it would be beneficial to start the structured conversation process early. A particularly useful access strategy in this case would be asking an effective communicator in the class, a pupil with particularly strong literacy skills, to act as a buddy for Karim. This will not only provide a model of the mathematical processes being learnt, it will help his language development and also his social integration. For further ideas try the National Association for Language Development in the Curriculum (NALDIC) website at http://www.naldic.org.uk.

Sexual orientation

CASE STUDY

Rhian's story: inclusive practice and preventing homophobia

A trainee teacher had the following two events occur during her second school experience.

I was placed in a reception class, and as part of my planning I wanted to read a lovely fairy tale with a twist called 'King and King'. My class teacher hadn't heard of the book, so asked me to bring it in. She read it through and then said it wasn't appropriate for her class to be reading things like that as they were only reception. I had no choice but to change the book, even though I knew that some of the children were likely to know a gay or lesbian couple and the book dealt with the issue sensitively and with humour.

As part of my experience I also spent time with Year 6, when I overheard a pupil call another 'gay'. I told the class teacher, who immediately had a circle time about the inappropriate use of the term. Several children shared stories of gay relatives and friends of the family, and the class was left in no doubt that homophobia would not be tolerated.

A parent had this simultaneous experience with her son's nursery teacher:

Early in the term we were asked to provide key dates for the family (birthdays, weddings, major family events) so the children could make cards etc. in class. I let the teacher know that my sister was having a civil partnership ceremony the following month, and that they would really appreciate a card from their nephew.

The Friday before the partnership ceremony I was told they 'hadn't got round' to making the card; I was left with the distinct impression they didn't approve and so had made the decision not to make the time for it. It raised serious questions for me regarding my child attending a school where such attitudes came from the staff.

Critical questions

» What do you think were the class teacher's main objections to Rhian's choice of text? Were they justified?

» What would be the benefits of sharing this kind of story with younger children?

» How visible are gay, lesbian, bisexual and transgender people in the media? In the local community? How might this be affecting the pupils' perceptions of what it means to be gay or lesbian, for example?

» *If you were teaching the child who has an aunt in a civil partnership, how would you have dealt with the issue of the card? What reason might the setting have had for not completing the activity? What message would the pupils be taking from this incident, particularly if other children were encouraged to make cards for relatives getting married?*

Extended thinking

» *In order to teach inclusively, what professional development might you require?*

» *Where might you source this professional development?*

» *What other demographics might you come across when teaching?*

Much of the public debate around sexual orientation and schools has centred incorrectly on issues of sex education, but particularly in primary schools the issue is one of inclusion. In 2009 the lesbian, gay and bisexual charity Stonewall published *The Teachers' Report*, which identified the teachers' perspective regarding homophobia and for the first time included primary schools in the data. It included many anecdotes of homophobic language going unchallenged due to poor staff confidence in dealing with the issue. The key issue identified by the research was the fact that homophobic bullying affected all children: pupils in schools were being taunted and abused using homophobic language, but often it was unrelated to their own sexual orientation.

With the introduction of civil partnerships and the current debate around marriage for gay and lesbian couples it is increasingly likely that you will teach a child with gay parents; like those from different ethnic groups and cultures they will wish to be seen, heard and valued. There are an increasing number of books and resources which can be used to encourage an inclusive approach:

*   The *Family Diversities Reading Resource* (Morris and Woolley, 2008) is a bibliography of children's literature that covers a range of issues including same-sex relationships.

*   Stonewall have developed a primary resource pack which celebrates different families and encourages a zero-tolerance approach to all forms of bullying, including homophobia: http://www.stonewall.org.uk/at_school/education_for_all/quick_links/education_resources/primary_school_resources/default.asp.

*   Other charities, such as the Lesbian and Gay Foundation (LGF), have also produced educational packs and resources which can be used for staff training as well as informed lesson planning.

*   Students at the University of Worcester have developed an online repository of information and helpful materials which can help create a positive classroom culture, which can be found at http://www.worcester.ac.uk/discover/education-creating-positive-classroom-cultures.html.

Chapter reflections

What should now be apparent is that children are diverse, and have diverse needs in the classroom environment. In order to develop your understanding of the range of factors that can inhibit pupils' ability to learn, it is useful to consider the key SEN terms and concepts you might come across in your school setting, but it is also important to think about the day-to-day aspects of life that can affect our engagement, enthusiasm and ability. Even if the children in your current placement do not have a range of special educational needs, they are all still individuals who might need support or help at different times or in different curriculum areas for very different reasons.

Critical points

» *Be informed: read widely around the areas of diversity and inclusion in order to keep your knowledge and understanding current.*

» *Remember that inclusion is not just about teaching children with SEN: it is about recognising and celebrating diversity, and ensuring equality of access for all.*

» *Use specialist colleagues, both in school and as part of the wider network of professions, to help you address individual learning needs.*

» *Good home–school communication is vital and should help highlight positives as well as identify problems.*

» *Embed inclusive teaching into your practice from the start rather than viewing it as an 'add-on' to your lesson.*

» *Think about your choice of resources and ensure you are recognising and celebrating diversity in a range of different ways.*

» *Make your classroom a diversity-and SEN-friendly zone, not least through appropriate displays and access to specialist equipment: do the children who need left-handed scissors have equal access to them alongside the right-handed pairs?*

Taking it further

Corbett, J (2001) Teaching approaches which support inclusive education: a connective pedagogy. *British Journal of Special Education*, (28)1: 55–59.

Farrell, M (2009) *The Special Education Handbook: An A–Z Guide*. Abingdon: David Fulton.

Goepel, J Childerhouse, H and Sharpe, S (2015) *Inclusive Primary Teaching: A Critical Approach to Equality and Special Educational Needs* (Second Edition). Northwich: Critical Publishing.

Golding, K S, Templeton, S, Fain, J, Mills, C, Worrall, H, Roberts, N, Durrant, E and Frost, A (2012) *Observing Children with Attachment or Emotional Difficulties in School*. London: Jessica Kingsley Publishers.

Soan, S (2010) *Improving Outcomes for Looked-after Children: A Practical Guide to Raising Aspirations and Achievement*. London: Optimus Education.

9 Creative placements

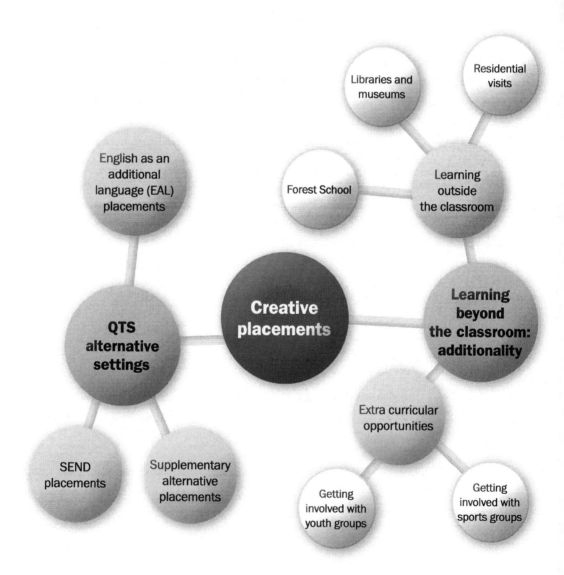

Teachers' Standards (DfE, 2011c)

1 Set high expectations which inspire, motivate and challenge pupils.

2 Promote good progress and outcomes by pupils.

3 Demonstrate good subject and curriculum knowledge.

4 Plan and teach well-structured lessons.

5 Adapt teaching to respond to the strengths and needs of all pupils.

6 Make accurate and productive use of assessment.

7 Manage behaviour effectively to ensure a good and safe learning environment.

8 Fulfil wider professional responsibilities.

Part Two: Personal and professional conduct

- Teachers uphold public trust in the profession and maintain high standards of ethics and behaviour, within and outside school, by:

    - treating pupils with dignity, building relationships rooted in mutual respect, and at all times observing proper boundaries appropriate to a teacher's professional position

    - having regard for the need to safeguard pupils' well-being, in accordance with statutory provisions

    - showing tolerance of and respect for the rights of others

    - not undermining fundamental British values, including democracy, the rule of law, individual liberty and mutual respect, and tolerance of those with different faiths and beliefs

    - ensuring that personal beliefs are not expressed in ways which exploit pupils' vulnerability or might lead them to break the law.

- Teachers must have proper and professional regard for the ethos, policies and practices of the school in which they teach, and maintain high standards in their own attendance and punctuality.

- Teachers must have an understanding of, and always act within, the statutory frameworks which set out their professional duties and responsibilities.

Introduction

Naturally you will want plenty of opportunities for practical teaching experience while you are training to be a teacher. As the old adage goes, 'Practice makes perfect'. Increasingly you will appreciate how the theory of teaching and learning relates to your everyday practice as your experience of teaching on your school placement advances. When choosing your training course, you might have been influenced by the length and variety of placements your provider could offer. What range of placements will you be exposed to while training?

In order to meet the Teaching Agency requirements (DfE, 2012d) you will be expected to work with age ranges immediately prior to and after the age phases you are training to teach. For example, if you are training to teach three to seven year olds, you are expected to undertake at least one visit to a setting catering for the birth to three years age group. Likewise if you are focusing on Key Stage 2 teaching, you will need to engage with a Year 1 or 2 class and a Year 7 class. Visits to high school can be achieved by accompanying the Year 6 class on their transition visit. You would not be obliged to teach the class, but if you are keen, enthusiastic and competent, the experience would enhance your practice as well as your CV. Obviously this would depend on the duration of your visit(s) and whether you can persuade the class teacher to hand the class over to you to teach!

This chapter considers alternative placements other than those in mainstream or independent primary settings. Some of the alternative placements will be staffed with qualified teaching professionals, whereas others will not; all, however, will:

- broaden your experience;
- contribute to your continuing professional development;
- prepare you to teach in a diverse society;
- improve your appreciation of inclusion;
- ultimately increase your employability potential and rating.

Due to the nature of the chapter, all Teachers' Standards are applicable; however, in some placement contexts certain standards will be more relevant and these are highlighted as appropriate.

Qualified Teacher Status (QTS) alternative settings

SEND placements

You may have a particular penchant and passion for working with children with special educational needs and disabilities (SEND). Many teacher training providers now facilitate a specialist pathway associated with SEND which will enable you to undertake placements in a SEND school. You may have a particular interest in teaching pupils with profound and multiple learning difficulties (PMLD); those with severe learning difficulties (SLD) and/or individuals with complex learning difficulties and disabilities (CLDD). You may already have conceived a future career aspiration to become a SENCO (Special Educational Needs Co-ordinator) and being exposed to this type of school placement would significantly enhance your chances of achieving your goal. Even for those who have no desire to work as a SENCO or at a special school, accessing this type of opportunity will open your eyes to different ways of working and provide you with additional skills that are transferable back into any mainstream setting. This is particularly useful and relevant since the changes to the SEND Code of Practice (DfE, 2015a) as discussed in Chapter 8.

CASE STUDY

Zahra's special school experience

I had signed up for the SEN pathway because prior to the course I had spent some time working in a SEND school. My first placement was in mainstream and I really enjoyed it but I know where my passion lies; I want to be teaching in a special school. The first thing I noticed was the small class sizes. I had eight pupils in my class. They were aged 12 and 14 but in terms of their actual attainment, they were working at levels between P2 and 3C. As you can imagine planning was interesting and so different from mainstream planning. I won't ever complain about having to plan for three different ability groups in mainstream again! One of the pupils, for example, had no verbal communication so used a communication switch. The thing I found quite challenging was that you were working with young adults (well, teenagers), some of whom exhibited teenage behaviours, and yet they were functioning at a level appropriate to an average pre-school child. Due to some of the learning difficulties, a couple of the pupils had quite challenging behaviour but I soon learned to follow their education, health and care (EHC) plans. I think that many trainees might find the number of adults you have in the class at one time overwhelming. In my class there were seven, including myself. When I first had to teach, I was scared stiff. Not because of the pupils but by the number of other adults – but they were great. Without the teaching assistants I couldn't have done my job; they are invaluable.

Critical questions

» How do you believe Zahra most benefited from her SEN placement?

» From the above report, which specific Teachers' Standards do you feel Zahra's SEND experience addressed well?

» In what ways would a SEND experience broaden a trainee teacher's experience?

» What personal skills and attributes do you think would be desirable for work in a SEND school?

» Potentially what positive impacts could this have on Zahra's mainstream teaching?

Comment on Zahra's special school experience

Due to the nature of SEND placements you will find that you work with smaller classes compared with mainstream settings. Clearly because of the various needs of the children you will be supported by a host of teaching assistants. Therefore a significant part of teaching in a SEND school is about being able to work as a team player and honing your collaborative skills. As Zahra highlights, planning is highly differentiated and personalised and included individual behaviour plans. This is in order to meet the individual needs of the pupils. Even for those of you who have no desire to teach long term in a special school, a short-term placement can help to enhance your understanding of key areas of teaching and learning as well as introduce you to the principles of the EHC plans that pupils with SEND need, regardless of the setting. In particular, Teachers' Standards 2, 5, 7 and 8 are covered thoroughly in a way that can provide ideas for how they might be achieved in mainstream schools.

To develop your knowledge and understanding of SEND, look at Chapter 8 and the Taking it further section at the end of this chapter.

English as an additional language (EAL) placements

Not all school placements will be enriched with pupils that have English as an additional language. Conversely, among the partnership schools involved with your training provider, there will be schools whose student population is formed almost entirely of young people whose first language is not English. If you find that you only have a short period of time visiting a school with EAL pupils, focus on how the teacher caters for this group and identify any areas of best practice. These might include the use of picture cues, simplified language or a mother-tongue teaching assistant. So what happens if you are placed in a school where there are no EAL pupils?

Lisa's story below charts a common issue that you may come across yourself while on practice. You are asked to consider the implications of such a situation and how you would resolve it.

CASE STUDY

Lisa's EAL experience

I had all my placements in classes where I had no EAL pupils, in fact the two school placements I had initially didn't have an EAL pupil in the whole school. There are a couple of EAL pupils here, but not in my class. So how am I supposed to know how to teach EAL pupils, let alone have confidence in my teaching if I've never taught them? The mentor thinks the same and has asked how on earth I am supposed to meet the standards?

Critical questions

» *What are the key issues facing Lisa?*

» *How might Lisa go about resolving these problems?*

» *Who would she need to involve in order to address the issues?*

» *How will Lisa know if she has been successful?*

» *Which Teachers' Standards would Lisa address if she were proactive, addressed the issues and took ownership of her own professional development?*

» *Ultimately, if you were Lisa's tutor what would you suggest for her key priority or developmental target against the Standards?*

» *How could the mentor be a better support to Lisa?*

» *Imagine you are the supervisory tutor assessing Lisa's situation. Using the question prompts from above and the table on the next page, draw up an action plan for Lisa.*

Issue or development point	Action to resolve issue or development point	Who is involved?	Success criteria	Teachers' Standards addressed

Extended thinking

» What literature or government publications would be useful in developing your knowledge of EAL?

» What are your top five tips for teaching EAL pupils effectively?

Comment on Lisa's EAL experience

Although Lisa is not immersed in a multitude of EAL pupils she is in a setting that has some EAL students. The first item on Lisa's action plan might be to arrange (through her mentor) an observation of the teacher in the class with EAL pupils. Lisa would do well to follow her observation with a professional dialogue with the teacher and the SENCO. Having accepted that Lisa could not meet the Standards due to the lack of EAL pupils, the mentor could have asked key probing questions in lesson feedback sessions. For example, the mentor might prompt Lisa to consider what she would do if there had been an EAL pupil in an observed lesson. How might she adapt her planning to reflect this? Would she arrange the pupils differently? What resources would she provide to cater for an EAL pupil? More significant, however, is Lisa's lack of reflection and her inability to be proactive in relation to her situation. Clearly Lisa's key priority for action is to be more reflective, and to take responsibility for her own continuing professional development in order to have a positive impact on her attainment and ability to meet the Standards.

Supplementary alternative placements

The two alternative settings mentioned above are those most commonly used for teaching placements due to the nature of the Teachers' Standards. There are, however, other settings that providers might work with as they can offer qualified teacher support. Having a qualified teaching professional who has undertaken the provider's custom-made mentor training will assure the provider that you will receive the quality of support you need in an alternative setting.

The coalition government (2010–15) relaxed the restrictions on the use of pupil referral units (PRUs) in teacher training. The use of pupil referral units was mentioned in relation to behaviour and classroom management in Chapter 5. You may want to consider exploring this opportunity with your provider as the government's notion for using these placement settings was to help support trainee teachers in the development of behaviour management: learning from the experts.

Additionally some providers may offer modern language placements abroad. This opportunity can provide you with an experience that takes you out of your comfort zone, placing you in a setting where you are immersed in your chosen language. As you can imagine, your language development is accelerated through this period and once again makes you stand out from the crowd when applying for teaching jobs.

Learning beyond the classroom: additionality

As discussed in Chapter 11, once you have completed your teacher training (or even before), you will apply for teaching jobs. It is at this point you may realise that, while you can wax lyrical about your experience of teaching phonics and mathematics, describe art and PE lessons in depth and explain the best methods for managing challenging behaviour, your letter of application lacks anything additional that will make you stand out from all the other newly qualified teachers applying for the same role. Of course head teachers and governing bodies want effective classroom practitioners, but it is important that you think about what other valuable skills and experience you can bring to a school.

Learning happens in a variety of situations outside of the classroom. By volunteering or working in other environments you will not only demonstrate a commitment to the holistic development of the child, but also foster skills not always enabled in the classroom environment.

CASE STUDY

Lorraine's out-of-school experience (part 1)

Part of my teacher training involved undertaking a five-day non-school placement in an environment where learning is taking place. We had to choose the placement and arrange it ourselves, but I didn't know where to start! My tutor directed me to a local charity that worked with young people around the county during weekends and school holidays, offering sports and art activities in quite deprived areas.

On the first day of half term I turned up and realised that no one knew exactly how many children would be arriving. I couldn't understand how it was going to work: in school we plan for a set number of children to do the same or similar activities, and here was a setting where numbers could change from morning to afternoon, and everyone who showed up effectively had free choice of the activities so there had to be several on offer.

Critical questions

» What are the implications of this sort of non-school placement for a) planning, b) resourcing and c) behaviour management?

» What skills, knowledge and understanding from her teacher training do you think Lorraine was able to utilise in this placement?

CASE STUDY

Lorraine's out-of-school experience (part 2)

Over the week I experienced the amount of planning, resourcing and commitment necessary to enable child-led activities; I also realised just how much I relied on classroom routines for things like behaviour management. Being in this environment made me much more confident when I went back in to school, but it also gave me a great opportunity as the charity is training me to be a paid play worker!

Critical questions

» *Why do you think Lorraine's confidence grew in her out-of-school experience?*

» *How else could an out-of-school experience benefit Lorraine?*

Extended thinking

» *What other possibilities might there be for 'out-of-school' experience?*

» *How would they develop your employability skills, attributes and attitudes?*

Comment on Lorraine's experience

In Lorraine's time with the charity she developed an understanding of child-led learning that she had not been able to experience in school outside of the Early Years environment. From this experience she was able to plan more opportunities for pupil choice. This kind of child-led practice does have serious implications for planning and preparation time, however, and by working with non-teaching organisations for whom this is a daily occurrence you can obtain valuable experience in how to manage this.

Learning outside the classroom

In 2006 the DfES produced the *Learning outside the Classroom* manifesto (DfES, 2006a), which is underpinned by the belief that every young person should experience the world beyond the classroom as an essential part of learning and personal development, whatever their age, ability or circumstances. Although subsequent changes in UK government have meant this is no longer part of the DfE agenda (the focus having switched to extended services) there is still a Council for Learning outside the Classroom (http://www.lotc.org.uk), which aims to promote out-of-school learning.

The Council for Learning outside the Classroom provides resources, guidance and CPD, including advice on curriculum design and policy, for teachers who wish to use the outdoor environment to enable learning. It builds upon the findings of the 2008 Ofsted report *Learning outside the Classroom: How Far Should You Go?* which stated that *When planned and implemented well, learning outside the classroom contributed significantly to raising standards and improving pupils' personal, social and emotional development.* This is still reflected in current policy through the Teachers' Standards where, in order to address

Standard 4, it is expected that teachers will *plan other out-of-class activities to consolidate and extend the knowledge and understanding pupils have acquired* (DfE, 2012f, page 8).

There are many ways that schools embed this into practice. The following sections discuss some of the most recognisable opportunities found in UK primary schools, but it is by no means a definitive list. *Outdoor Learning 2015*, an impact study led by the Institute for Outdoor Learning into current practice in the UK (as a systematic review of evidence), may provide you with further insight into effective provision for children and young people: further information can be found at http://www.outdoor-learning.org/Default.aspx?tabid=365&ld=729.

Forest School

The idea of Forest School originated in Sweden and has gained momentum in primary schools in the UK since 2000. It is based on the concept of encouraging and enabling play in the outdoors as a way of providing children with greater opportunities for creativity, independence and imagination. Alongside this is a wish to inspire an understanding of the natural environment and sustainable living.

There are independent and local authority-run Forest School centres throughout the UK, although many schools are now cultivating small woodland environments on site where space allows. A member of staff is trained as a Forest School leader: this does not have to be a member of the teaching staff, and will often be a higher level teaching assistant (HLTA). Forest School sessions might include elements of the curriculum but are far more child- and environment-led, focusing on life skills rather than academic ones.

Proponents of Forest School state that children given this opportunity are more confident, sociable and better behaved than those learning in more urban environments; research studies have identified 'that connections to nature can help to enhance understanding of the world we live in and are part of building connections with community and, in turn, developing a sense of belonging' (Nash and Cumming, 2015). There is also the view that all children, including those who have specific learning difficulties (SpLD), benefit from learning how to manage risks, rather than avoid them, in the outdoors.

CASE STUDY

Steven's story: Jordan and Forest School

Right from the start of my school placement with a Year 3 class I was aware of Jordan. His behaviour wasn't good: he would call out in class, refuse to join in group tasks and on bad days would end up fighting with someone in the class. The other children weren't keen to spend time with him, and would complain if they had to work with him.

After half term it was Year 3's turn to go to Forest School, which took place a short minibus ride away. Jordan was the first one to be dressed in the waterproof coverall and wellies needed for the trip; he waited patiently for the bus; and once in the woodland he appeared to be a different child! He assisted some of his classmates in building a den, and they all seemed to take much more notice of him in this environment. He was able to think much more practically and strategically than some of his more 'academic' peers. The class teacher said that right from starting school Jordan had struggled in the classroom, but excelled in the outdoors, which made me realise how important it was that children got the chance to experience learning outside the classroom.

Critical questions

» *Think about the range of life skills we want pupils in primary school to develop, for example communication skills, independence, self-awareness. How are they promoted in the classroom environment?*

» *What further opportunities are provided by the outdoors environment?*

» *How can Steven use this experience to plan effective lessons which include Jordan back at school?*

Comment on Steven's story

In Steven's case he was able to see Jordan in a different light and realise that the pupil was able to make significant progress in the right environment. While it was not possible to teach every lesson outside, Steven was able to make his lessons more multi-sensory and practical, enabling Jordan to engage in and enjoy the learning more.

Libraries and museums

During holiday periods most museums, heritage sites and libraries offer a families programme to encourage visitors. These events often require extra staff, and as a trainee teacher your skills are invaluable in supporting them. In return they will enable you to be more knowledgeable regarding the opportunities provided by the setting for school visits.

Public libraries are not the quiet places of study they once were. Children are actively encouraged to attend storytelling sessions or take part in book-related activities such as reading challenges or design competitions linked to texts. By volunteering or working alongside the librarians you will gain an understanding about how to promote reading and related literacy activities in an engaging way.

Museums and heritage sites will also value your training and provide you with an opportunity to develop skills, knowledge and understanding regarding historical and cultural artefacts. The Museums Association provides information about the sort of opportunities available to you (http://www.museumsassociation.org/careers/volunteering). By immersing yourself in this sort of learning experience you will not only be reminded of the importance of experiential, hands-on learning, but also gain an insight into the way historical artefacts are kept and stored in order to preserve them.

Critical questions

» *What do you know about the role of a librarian or historical curator?*

» *How might a voluntary role in a library or museum develop your skills as a trainee teacher? Think about the wider role as well as curriculum knowledge and try to complete the table below.*

Interpersonal Skills	Curriculum Subject Knowledge
•	•
•	•
•	•
•	•
•	•

Residential visits

School trips to residential centres provide a significant opportunity for learning outside the classroom, and as a trainee you may be invited to accompany a school, or even have the necessary qualifications to work in a centre when not studying. Outdoor education or activity centres can provide opportunities for physical activities not possible in most school environments, such as sailing or rock climbing, and visits to other parts of the country, or indeed other countries, can give children a greater social understanding. However, it must be noted that it is more likely to be of value to pupils when it is successfully embedded as part of long-term curriculum planning. Ofsted (2006, page 5) found that

Too many residential and other visits considered during the survey had learning objectives which were imprecisely defined and not integrated sufficiently with activities in the classroom. This was particularly the case in primary schools.

It is important, then, to evaluate the experience you are being offered in order to see if you can identify the intended curriculum links.

Extra-curricular opportunities

Not all learning is linked to school, and many children are members of clubs and groups that take place in the evenings and weekends. When on placement you may be asked to run an after-school club, and again having experience of an extra-curricular setting can provide you with an indispensable skill set.

Getting involved with youth groups

Many communities have a youth centre or use of a local school building in the evenings for clubs and societies. For example, the Scouts and Guides Associations are charitable groups which offer many opportunities for learning through diverse activities, and it is only through the participation of adult volunteers that they are able to provide these events and experiences. Church groups and youth clubs also rely on volunteers. By joining organisations such as these you will gain non-curriculum planning experience, potential leadership experience and in some cases qualifications such as first aid training that will enhance your CV while you make a contribution to the wider community.

Getting involved with sports groups

Junior football leagues supported by the Football Association, swimming clubs affiliated to British Swimming and the ASA, accredited athletics clubs and so on all provide opportunities to work with pupils in a variety of ways. You may feel you do not have the sporting ability to be involved, but sports clubs for young people often need administrative support, treasurers, child protection officers and other such individuals not necessarily involved in training. If you are interested in gaining a coaching qualification then the associated bodies are able to provide this.

CASE STUDY

Annie's story

I was a regular volunteer at my children's swimming club long before I began teacher training. I was in a seminar one day when the debate about effective teaching got quite heated: I have to admit it was me that was getting frustrated! I couldn't understand why the tutor was saying that learning might not always be creative and child-led, as this seemed to be the best way to me. I had made reference to my coaching experience in the past and the tutor asked me to describe a typical session in the pool. As I ran through what normally happens I realised that swimming lessons are not usually 'creative' in the way I had been arguing for; in fact the sessions can be quite directive or inductive rather than exploratory, and yet effective learning was still taking place. I realised, then, that I needed to make more use of my expertise from outside of the classroom to support my own development as a teacher.

Critical questions

» What other settings (apart from those already discussed) offer opportunities for learning outside of the classroom?

» Do you think it is important for a teacher to experience learning outside of the classroom? Try to justify your response by linking it to your educational values: what do you believe the purpose of school to be?

Chapter reflections

Placement variety is the 'spice' of your teaching life! Diverse placement experiences will help to enrich your teaching as you engage with learning new skills and knowledge. In turn, your lessons will be more interesting, well-managed and resourced. Alternative placements have the potential to make you a more self-assured and balanced teacher. Engage with broader placement contexts and see your confidence and employability prospects grow.

Critical points

» Seek out the opportunities and challenges that an alternative placement can bring.

» Be open to different ways of working.

» Diverse placements can open up different employment opportunities.

» Take ownership of your career development from the outset.

Taking it further

Advanced training materials for autism, dyslexia, speech, language and communication, emotional, social and behavioural difficulties and moderate learning difficulties. www.education.gov.uk/lamb/.

Institute for Outdoor Learning: member website http://www.outdoor-learning.org/Default.aspx?tabid=68.

Knight, S (2009) *Forest Schools and Outdoor Learning in the Early Years*. London: Sage.

Knight, S (2011) *Forest School for All*. London: Sage.

Lamb Inquiry: *Special Educational Needs and Parental Confidence*. www.education.gov.uk/publications/eOrderingDownload/01143–2009DOM-EN.pdf.

Salt Review: Independent Review of Teacher Supply for Pupils with Severe, Profound and Multiple Learning Difficulties. www.education.gov.uk/publications/eOrderingDownload/00195–2010BKT-EN.pdf.

Training materials for teaching SEND students. www.education.gov.uk/complexneeds/.

Waite, S (ed.) (2011) *Children Learning outside the Classroom from Birth to Eleven*. London: Sage.

10 From good to outstanding

Introduction

Defining what is meant by outstanding in the context of teaching is problematic for a plethora of reasons. Teaching is not an exact science, rather it is woven with intricacies and complexities, complicated further by the subjective nature of making a professional judgement about what makes teaching outstanding. With the introduction in 2012 of one set of Teachers' Standards (DfE, 2012f) for all teachers, the blurred expectations combined with the idiosyncratic nature of assessing teachers has made the job of identifying best practice all the more challenging. The interpretative guidance set out in the Standards states that the:

new standards will need to be applied as appropriate to the role and context within which a trainee or teacher is practising. Providers of Initial Teacher Training (ITT) will assess trainees against the Standards in a way that is consistent with what could reasonably be expected of a trainee teacher prior to the award of QTS.

So what of those trainee teachers who are deemed to be outstanding practitioners, what do these individuals radiate? What do you do to move from being classed as a good trainee teacher to an outstanding one?

Previous assessment criteria devised by Ofsted for trainee teachers provide an excellent starting point for identifying performance in four main areas of practice. The four areas are:

*   lessons;
*   paperwork;
*   professional discussions;
*   noticeable features.

These criteria can be used to very good effect prior to starting a final placement, perhaps as a self-assessment tool. Alternatively, you might evaluate your performance with your mentor or college tutor collaboratively. Whatever the assessment strategy used to identify the level of your performance, the outcome will give rise to next steps for learning, and challenging yet achievable targets will be set for your final placement. Most recently Ofsted (2015) state that to be deemed outstanding:

All primary … trainees awarded QTS exceed the minimum level of practice expected of teachers as defined in the Teachers' Standards by the end of their training. Trainees demonstrate excellent practice in the majority of the standards for teaching and all related to their personal and professional conduct. Much of their teaching is outstanding and never less than consistently good. (p 34)

Interestingly, in the latest Ofsted inspection framework for ITE (Ofsted, 2015), no trainee teacher can be found to be working at a pass level or requiring improvement (Ofsted terminology) if the provider is to be judged outstanding. There is increasing pressure on you to attain at a good or better level and this chapter seeks to assist you in accomplishing these higher levels of attainment. The chapter highlights the traits of a good and an outstanding trainee teacher and provides you with informative criteria for each stage of your professional development. It is hoped that you use this chapter to engage in critical self-reflection and consequently identify your next steps in learning so that you complete your training at an outstanding level.

Good versus outstanding

A good trainee

You are now likely to be working at a good level in terms of your teaching and hopefully have aspirations to be an outstanding trainee teacher. First consider the table below to determine if you are working at a good level. Attaining at a good level is almost a prerequisite for achieving outstanding by the end of your school placements.

Critical questions

» *Take a highlighter pen and highlight each criterion in the table below that you believe you meet at a good level.*

» *What examples can you give to support your selection?*

» *Which criteria are you not achieving at a good level? Why? What barriers are there to you achieving good in these areas? How will you address these in the first instance?*

Teachers' Standards	A good trainee will:	An outstanding trainee will:
1 Set high expectations which inspire, motivate and challenge pupils	reliably encourage pupils to participate and contribute in an atmosphere conducive to learning; set high expectations of pupils in their different training contexts; consistently demonstrate professional behaviour; be well respected by pupils and effectively promote pupils' resilience, confidence and independence when tackling challenging activities. As a result of this most pupils are enthused and motivated to participate.	constantly encourage pupils to participate and contribute in an atmosphere highly conducive to learning; consistently have high expectations of pupils in different training contexts; have high levels of mutual respect between the trainee and pupils; be very effective in promoting pupils' resilience, confidence and independence when tackling challenging activities; generate high levels of enthusiasm, participation and commitment to learning.
2 Promote good progress and outcomes by pupils	assume responsibility for the attainment, progress and outcomes of the pupils they teach; demonstrate a sound understanding of the need to develop pupil learning over time;	assume a high level of responsibility for the attainment progress and outcomes of the pupils they teach;

Teachers' Standards	A good trainee will:	An outstanding trainee will:
	consistently take into account the prior learning of the pupils when planning in the short and medium term; regularly provide pupils with the opportunity to reflect on their own learning and use this, along with other forms of assessment, to inform their future planning and teaching; use their knowledge of effective teaching strategies to encourage independent learning and set appropriately challenging tasks which enable the pupils to make progress. As a result the majority of pupils make good progress.	demonstrate confident judgement in planning for pupil progression both within individual lessons and over time and are able to articulate a clear and well-justified rationale as to how they are building on prior achievement; actively promote engaging and effective methods that support pupils in reflecting on their learning; set appropriately challenging tasks, drawing on a secure knowledge of the pupils' prior attainment which has been obtained through systematic and accurate assessment; regularly create opportunities for independent and autonomous learning. As a result the majority of pupils make very good progress.
3 Demonstrate good subject and curriculum knowledge	have well-developed knowledge and understanding of the relevant subject/ curriculum areas they are training to teach and use this effectively to maintain and develop pupils' interest; make good use of their secure curriculum and pedagogical subject knowledge to deepen pupils' knowledge and understanding, addressing common errors and misconceptions effectively in their teaching; be critically aware of the need to extend and update their subject, curriculum and pedagogical knowledge and know how to employ appropriate professional development strategies to further develop these in their early career;	draw on their in-depth subject and curriculum knowledge to plan confidently for progression and to stimulate and capture pupils' interest; demonstrate very well-developed pedagogical subject knowledge, by anticipating common errors and misconceptions in their planning; be astutely aware of their own development needs in terms of extending and updating their subject, curriculum and pedagogical knowledge in their early career and have been proactive in developing these effectively during their training;

Teachers' Standards	A good trainee will:	An outstanding trainee will:
	model good standards of written and spoken communication in all professional activities and encourage and support pupils to develop these skills in their lessons.	model very high standards of written and spoken communication in all professional activities. They successfully identify and exploit opportunities to develop pupils' skills, in communication, reading and writing;
		in relation to early reading, draw on their very strong understanding of synthetic systematic phonics and its role in teaching and assessing reading and writing to teach literacy very effectively across the age phases they are training to teach; in relation to early mathematics, draw on their very strong knowledge and understanding of the principles and practices of teaching early mathematics to select and employ highly effective teaching strategies across the age ranges they are training to teach.
4 Plan and teach well-structured lessons	show a willingness to try out a range of approaches to teaching and learning; plan lessons that take account of the needs of groups of pupils and individuals, through the setting of differentiated learning outcomes, carefully matching teaching and learning activities and resources to support pupils in achieving these intended learning outcomes; understand how homework or other out-of-class work can sustain pupils' progress and consolidate learning and can design and set appropriate tasks; know how to learn from both successful and less effective lessons through their systematic evaluation of the effectiveness of their practice, including its impact on pupils; make a positive contribution to the development of curriculum and resources in their placement settings.	plan lessons that often use well-chosen imaginative and creative strategies and that match individuals' needs and interests; be highly reflective in critically evaluating their practice; accurately judge the impact of their practice on individuals and groups of pupils and can use their evaluation to inform future planning, teaching and learning; show initiative in contributing to curriculum planning and developing and producing effective learning resources in their placement settings.

Teachers' Standards	A good trainee will:	An outstanding trainee will:
5 Adapt teaching to respond to the strengths and needs of all pupils	consistently adapt their teaching to meet the needs of individual and groups of pupils to support progression in learning; know how to secure progress for pupils and how to identify when groups and individuals have made progress; have a range of effective strategies that they can apply to reduce barriers and respond to the strengths and needs of their pupils; clearly recognise how to deal with any potential barriers to learning through their application of well-targeted interventions and the appropriate deployment of available support staff.	quickly and accurately discern their pupils' strengths and needs and be proactive in differentiating and employing a range of effective intervention strategies to secure progression for individuals and groups; have an astute understanding of how effective different teaching approaches are in terms of impact on learning and engagement of pupils.
6 Make accurate and productive use of assessment	be able to assess pupils' attainment accurately against national benchmarks; employ a range of appropriate formative assessment strategies effectively and adapt their teaching within lessons in light of pupils' responses; maintain accurate records of pupils' progress and use these to set appropriately challenging targets; assess pupils' progress regularly and accurately and discuss assessments with them so that pupils know how well they have done and what they need to do to improve.	confidently and accurately assess pupils' attainment against national benchmarks; use a range of assessment strategies very effectively in their day-to-day practice to monitor progress and to inform future planning; systematically and effectively check pupils' understanding throughout lessons, anticipating where intervention may be needed and do so with notable impact on the quality of learning; assess pupils' progress regularly and work with them to accurately target further improvement and secure rapid progress.
7 Manage behaviour effectively to ensure a good and safe learning environment	work within the school's framework for behaviour and apply rules and routines consistently and fairly;	rapidly adapt to the different circumstances in which they train, working confidently within the frameworks established in different settings and applying rules and routines consistently and fairly;

Teachers' Standards	A good trainee will:	An outstanding trainee will:
	consistently have high expectations and understand a range of strategies that experienced teachers use to promote positive behaviour and apply these effectively, including use of school sanctions and rewards and use of praise, in order to create an environment supportive of learning; manage behaviour effectively so that pupils demonstrate positive attitudes towards the teacher, their learning and each other allowing lessons to flow smoothly so that disruption is unusual; actively seek additional support in addressing the needs of pupils where significantly challenging behaviour is demonstrated.	manage pupil behaviour with ease so that pupils display very high levels of engagement, courtesy, collaboration and cooperation.
8 Fulfil wider professional responsibilities	be proactive in seeking out opportunities to contribute to the wider life and ethos of the school; be effective in building good professional relationships with colleagues and demonstrate that they can work well collaboratively when required to do so; take responsibility for deploying support staff in their lessons and for seeking advice from relevant professionals in relation to pupils with individual needs; be proactive in terms of their own professional learning and value the feedback they receive from more experienced colleagues, using it to develop their own teaching further; communicate effectively, both verbally and in writing, with parents and carers in relation to pupils' achievements and well-being. They assume some responsibility for doing so in response to individual pupils' emergent needs.	be proactive in seeking out opportunities to contribute in a significant way to the wider life and ethos of the school; build strong professional relationships and demonstrate that they are able to work collaboratively with colleagues on a regular basis; deliberately seek out opportunities to develop their own professional learning and respond positively to all the feedback they receive; communicate very effectively, both verbally and in writing, with parents and carers in relation to pupils' achievements and well-being, both when required to do so formally and are proactive in communicating in relation to individual pupils' emergent needs.

Competencies for trainee teachers, based on UCET/NASBTT & HEA 2012

Now that you have identified your current achievement based on honest self-reflection, you need to consider how you will take the next steps to become a truly outstanding teacher. In order to do this, you will need to consider what is meant by outstanding and how to move from good to outstanding.

Extended thinking

» *The Teachers' Standards (DfE, 2012f) Part 1 focuses on Teaching; however there is a Part 2 which outlines the expectations of a teacher's personal and professional conduct. Find and read the statements found in Part 2: what are the implications for you as a trainee teacher?*

» *How can teachers demonstrate consistently high standards of personal and professional conduct in order to meet the standards in Part 2?*

What makes an outstanding trainee?

Being outstanding is not something that happens solely in a one-off lesson. You could put on a *great big show* (Paton, 2012) for an observed lesson; something that the now chief of Ofsted, Michael Wilshaw, emphatically detests. For you to stand out as outstanding you will need to reliably exhibit commitment and consistency in your personal attributes and professional physiognomies. You should be steadfast in the degree to which you are highly motivated and devoted to your teaching performance and the progress of all your pupils. For instance you should be able to demonstrate an ability to be flexible and change your teaching to suit the pace and knowledge of your pupils. Putting on a seamless performance, throwing caution to the wind in terms of your planning (when appropriate) and going with what the pupils require all play a part in your ability to be outstanding. Likewise if things go wrong (which they have a tendency to do on occasions) you should have the ability to critically reflect on your feet (in action) and make adaptations immediately in a lesson. Often these adaptations and decisions are made inherently because it feels right. There are no set formulae to follow in a given situation; it just comes instinctively due to your ability to reflect in a given situation.

An outstanding trainee

Be consistent

The Teachers' Standards (DfE, 2012f) along with UCET and NASBTT guidance (2012) plainly outline what constitutes outstanding in terms of your performance as a trainee teacher. For you to be considered as an 'outstanding' or 'higher' trainee at the end of your programme of ITE you will have to meet the Teachers' Standards (DfE, 2012f) at both a pass and a good level and may have additionally demonstrated the skills and attributes outlined in the table above. However, for you to be deemed outstanding you do not need to display all of the outstanding competencies, all of the time. The UCET and NASBTT (2012, page 4) support materials plainly state that:

'Outstanding' achievement is an overall judgement. In a best fit model, the statements describe indicative additional features of practice that are characteristic of a trainee performing at that level. They also

need to be interpreted within the setting and context in which the trainee has worked. Trainees graded as 'outstanding' teach consistently good lessons that often demonstrate outstanding features across a range of different contexts (for example, different ages, backgrounds, group sizes, and abilities) by the end of their training.

Act incisively

One of the key skills you should have as an outstanding teacher is the ability to act incisively. This is often related to dealing with behaviour. You should respond rapidly when situations arise in your classroom and not dawdle, waiting for someone to step in to assist if a child's behaviour veers towards the dangerous. Alternatively, you know the children well enough to nip the behaviour in the bud with a quiet word before the pupil goes into meltdown. Chapter 5 gives some clear guidance on how to deal with behaviour, so if you are still not confident in this area, you might like to review that chapter.

Be proactive

Being highly proactive will not only get you noticed, it will drive your professional development forward at a more rapid pace. For example, if you purposefully seek out advice from an experienced teacher and actually put their advice into practice, this will be looked upon favourably. Equally if you volunteer to run an extra-curricular club or start a project that can be continued after you have left, these will all assist you in making the leap to being outstanding. Jenny recounts her project experience as a trainee teacher in her final placement below. (For information about story sacks, see the Taking it further section at the end of the chapter.)

CASE STUDY

Jenny's project

I was in my final placement and things were hectic as I was teaching 80 per cent of the time, however I wondered if I could get a project off the ground at the school. I thought it would benefit the pupils in the first instance but it similarly assisted me in terms of how I achieved on that final placement. I was daunted by the prospect of approaching the head teacher but kept telling myself, the worst that could happen was to be told I could not go ahead with my plan. So I bit the bullet and asked the head if I could start a story sack project involving myself and the parents. The head was in agreement so I set about writing a letter to parents across the school. The head checked the letter and I sent it out. The response from parents was fantastic and we held our first meeting a week later. Each parent shared their ideas and we decided to make three story sacks each containing traditional English activities. In addition we went one step further and incorporated some maths activities as well. I had been at a staff meeting on my first day of placement where we looked at the school's progress against the targets detailed on the school development plan (SDP). I thought the story sacks might assist in meeting some of the targets for the school. As a teacher (albeit a trainee teacher) I had my part to play in making a difference to the children's education at the school and knew it was my duty to offer assistance in any way I could. The parents went away and searched cupboards for material to make the bags while I looked at appropriate English and maths activities that could be incorporated.

The outcome was that by the end of the placement we had three story sacks that children were using in their lessons across the school. The children were highly engaged with the maths activities in particular and class teachers commented on the impact they were having on the pupils' attainment; I was delighted. I had another meeting with the parents later in my placement to plan the next few story sacks and I was able to leave the school knowing that the project initiative I had started was sustainable owing to the high levels of participation and investment from both parents and the school.

Critical questions

» What facets of Jenny's practice would you deem as outstanding?

» Consider your own practice: have you a project idea? How will you set about getting it off the ground? What assistance might you need?

Comment on Jenny's project

While it was obviously a bit daunting for Jenny to speak to the head teacher about her idea, she plucked up the courage to have the initial conversation. The outcome was rewarding not only for the pupils but also for the parents and the wider school community, and resulted in Jenny contributing significantly to whole school targets. Ultimately this project along with other aspects of her practice resulted in Jenny being judged as outstanding.

Take responsibility

Crucially, you need to take responsibility. It is not acceptable to apportion culpability to others, give excuses or ignore the broader role you have as a teacher. We all make mistakes or do not deliver on occasions, but you need to stand back, reflect and think about what you could do differently next time. At a very simple level, enquire if you can bring the pupils in from the playground each morning, settle the children in class and take the register. This demonstrates your commitment to teaching and to the pupils within your class. You will go a long way in showing the children (and parents) that you are a class teacher by walking the walk and shouldering the responsibilities that come with the job. A telling sign of whether you have been successful in your endeavour is if parents start to discuss concerns with you as a matter of course. While not necessarily the most pleasant aspect of the job, it signals that they accept you as the teacher and that you have achieved their respect.

Beginning to action change

Critical questions

» Review the table on pages 135–139 and the above points made in relation to being outstanding. What are the fundamental aspects that identify an outstanding trainee teacher?

» What makes an outstanding trainee stand out from the crowd?

» In which areas do you consider yourself as outstanding?

» Identify elements of your practice that you currently do not exhibit or need to improve *and list them in the table below to create an action plan. These developmental points are addressed later in the chapter.*

Outstanding competency to develop (Issue)	How will you develop this skill/competency? (Action)	When will you develop this? (Timescale)	Who will identify that you achieved your target? (People involved)	How will you know you have been successful? (Success criteria)

Hopefully you now have a clearer idea of what constitutes outstanding in a trainee teacher, and the areas in which you need to further develop. It is essential therefore that you begin to engage with your action plan above and consider how you will move your practice from good to achieving your goal of outstanding.

How to move from good to outstanding

Sam's story encapsulates the transition from being considered as a good trainee teacher to becoming an outstanding one. Read his story with careful consideration as you will be asked to identify and evaluate the key skills, competencies and attitudes he has demonstrated.

CASE STUDY

Sam's good to outstanding story

I was consistently getting graded as a good teacher by my mentor in my last placement. I was a bit disappointed, to be frank, as in my second placement (which I completed in a SEN school) I was rated as outstanding. I know now that the expectations for my second school placement were not as high and the context was also very different. I was soon to be visited by my supervisory tutor from the university and I wanted to make a really good impression but didn't know quite how to go about changing my fortunes to become outstanding in my mainstream setting.

My tutor was going to watch a number of lessons over the course of my placement so I needed to consistently perform at an outstanding level. I decided therefore to arrange a meeting with my academic tutor back at university, someone who knew me really well and that I believed could help solve my conundrum. My academic tutor was brilliant! She sat me down and started to brainstorm ideas for delivering a lesson that I was to conduct later that week on comparative and superlative adjectives with my Year 3/4 mixed class. I just couldn't see how I was going to make it exciting whereby children completed activities other than worksheets. I knew my academic tutor had a similar dislike for worksheets so I hoped that between us we could come up with some suggestions for creative pupil activities. Well, what a plan I ended up with. My class were grouped according to a Jamaican theme as my class teacher was Jamaican, so this information gave me a context in which to set the lesson – Jamaica! One activity that my academic tutor suggested was using exotic fruits as a starting point and to write comparative/superlative adjectives on large white tablecloths. I designed menus that children had to complete (much more engaging than a boring worksheet). All the children loved writing on the tablecloths and this provided me with an excellent assessment opportunity.

The mentor was blown away by the lesson and I was graded as outstanding. The key to the success of my lesson was down to the fact I had children at the heart of my creative planning and delivery. I was conscious, however, that I had to keep this up. With my tutor coming in to see a music lesson (not the strongest of my subjects in terms of subject knowledge, but one I really like teaching) I met my academic tutor once more. The time spent with her was time well spent as she is a specialist in primary music so was able to clarify my creative ideas, which included the use of technology. My academic tutor really liked the lesson I had planned but she raised a really pertinent point in relation to children improving their musical compositions. I wanted them to perform and appraise their animal sound compositions, stating what they liked about their own compositions and what they would improve on. My academic tutor questioned how the children might do that when music was not like any other subject; once performed it disappears into the ether unlike a story written in a book! This got me thinking quite rightly about recording the performances and playing them back to the class. I carried this out in my lesson, and again it worked brilliantly. The children were fantastic self-critics and made huge improvements to their compositions on hearing their original performances. My supervisory tutor graded my lesson as outstanding. I knew that I had now got the confidence to know what to do to make my lessons and overall performance consistently outstanding.

Critical questions

» List the key professional attributes Sam exhibits.

» What elements of the Teachers' Standards did Sam meet at the outstanding level according to the table on pages 130–134?

» Were there any calculated risks made in either of his lessons?

» In what ways was Sam creative?

CASE STUDY

Adam's good to outstanding story

I was undertaking my final placement in a Welsh school as I ultimately wanted to be employed in Wales. The experience was amazing as the curriculum is skills-based and very different from England's. I also had to teach some incidental Welsh which was a challenge as I didn't really speak very much myself. My mentor and the school were so supportive, I loved it there. I decided that I'd like to run an ICT club, which I got off the ground, and it was soon noticed that I was quite good with technology. I then started to think that I needed to use it more in my day-to-day teaching. My supervisory tutor said how creative my resources were for lessons, and in particular I was congratulated on the use of my personal iPad in a science lesson. I had linked the iPad to the IWB and had the children scribing through the iPad their own thoughts about magnetism onto a large mind map at the start of the magnet topic I was teaching. The potential for using technology creatively is immense and my mentor was in awe of this. I volunteered to run some drop-in informal teacher development sessions for the staff after school in the use of technology, and particularly the iPad, as there were 15 available in the school. The staff were delighted and I had regular attendees so was able to deliver a short tailored programme of CPD for the remaining time I was in my placement.

Critical questions

»   Adam took a number of risks on his final placement. What risks can you identify?

»   How has Adam moved from being good to outstanding?

»   What was significant about his practice that justified 'outstanding'?

»   Look back at the action plan you created. What additional challenging targets must you set in order to steer yourself along the path to outstanding?

Chapter reflections

Be honest with yourself in terms of reflecting on your practice. Reflection is key to you achieving outstanding status. If you get your reflection right along with your actions, you have the potential to be outstanding! To be considered outstanding you need to inspire, include and innovate. Ultimately you need to make a significant positive impact on pupils. Ask yourself, have you made a difference to the lives of those you are teaching? Have the pupils attained highly since you have been teaching them? Have you had a positive impact on the pupils, school and wider community? If the answer to any of these questions is no, what do you intend to do about it?

Critical points

»   Become a thespian in the classroom – no matter what is going on in your personal life you need to put on an act in the classroom; every day is a new performance!

»   Be proactive.

»   Take responsibility.

»   Seek out advice and take ownership of your continuing professional development.

» *Take risks.*

» *Go the extra mile.*

» *Always reflect on your practice and make adjustments accordingly.*

Taking it further

McBer, H DfES (2000) *Research into Teaching Effectiveness: A Model of Teacher Effectiveness.* London: DfEE.

National Literacy Trust. *Early Reading Connects: Story Sacks.* www.literacytrust.org.uk/assets/0000/3210/Story_sack_guide.pdf.

11 Employability

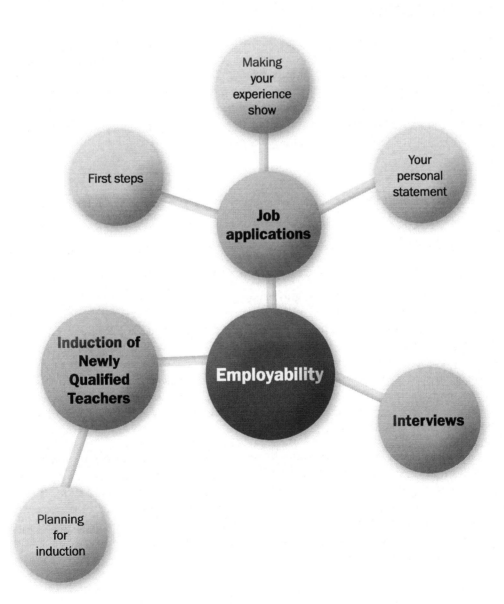

Introduction

Throughout your college career the course that you have been on will have equipped you with the necessary skills and practice, as outlined in the Teachers' Standards (DfE, 2011c), in order that you may ultimately reach Qualified Teacher Status (QTS). It now only remains for you to get your first job in order that you may start your induction period as a newly qualified teacher. This will allow you an opportunity to further develop your own professional practice while being supported and guided by the school's mentoring programme in order for you to reach a successful conclusion to this very important and necessary start to your professional career. So how do you best go about securing this first step towards your future chosen occupation?

Job applications

While at college you will need to begin to start thinking about, and then applying for, your first job. This will come around very quickly for you during your last year at college so it is important that you should start thinking about where you wish to work, what age of children you prefer to teach and the type of setting in which you would like to work. In addition to this, think about how you are going to be able to manage any home/life commitments you currently have as well as taking on a teaching job. Your first teaching post is very important, so it is vital that you reflect upon this commitment before you make any decisions or put in any applications.

Critical questions

» *What type of age range, school and geographical area might you wish to apply for?*

» *What do you think you can offer any school before you make an application?*

» *What commitments have you currently got that could affect an application?*

Any advertisements for jobs starting in September will begin to appear in the spring and summer terms and be placed by individual schools. Keep checking internal county vacancies sheets, relevant websites, such as the Times Educational Supplement (TES), and local and national press advertisements for vacancies. You may also register for updates on teaching posts from websites such as Eteach (www.eteach.com). Always remember that your university careers centre is there to help and guide you. They can give you information on the publications they have available that may help you in your search for employment. You may also be alerted to potential vacancies by your school of education, tutors or even schools in which you have had placements.

When you apply for a vacancy you will receive an information pack from the local authority (LA) or from an individual school about the post. It will normally contain details regarding the application process, an application form and associated documentation, the person specification, job specification, safeguarding policy and a prospectus. The pack will also contain a reminder that the school is committed to safeguarding those in their care and a statement that all employees are required to undertake a check with the Disclosure and Barring Service (DBS).

First steps

The school you apply to may suggest you contact them for further details or to request a visit. Use this as an opportunity to show your face and to make a good impression. Remember, if you have been to a school it helps them to make a link between you as a person and your application form. It also shows you value them enough to give up your time to visit them. The other benefit for you is that it will give you a chance to see if you like the idea of working in such a setting and to ask questions about it in order to clarify issues left unanswered from reading the application form. You must arrange a time to visit a school; don't just turn up. Schools are very busy places and just turning up will not create a good impression. It might be that there are times already allocated for you to look around the school. Whatever the case, try to find time to visit if at all possible. However, be realistic! Think about whether it is feasible for you to miss time from placements or university and whether it is too distant to visit anyway. Most schools will understand if you just email or write and explain why you are unable to visit.

CASE STUDY

John's story

Consider the following case in which a head teacher recalls showing John (a trainee teacher) around his school with other prospective applicants. The head teacher recalled that:

John seemed a nice enough student, however he seemed very quiet compared to the others in the group I showed around. I hardly noticed him. He said very little and hardly asked any questions. He didn't really talk to any pupils when he met them. It was hard to get to know what he was like. He was not as forthcoming as some of the others and I found it hard to know if he would fit into my team.

Critical questions

»   *What more could John have done to project his personality?*

»   *What sort of questions could John have asked?*

»   *How could he have reacted to the staff and pupils he met?*

»   *How could John have demonstrated that he would fit into the school team?*

Comment on John's story

John needed to ensure he spoke up more and didn't let others dominate. He needed to give non-verbal clues that he was interested in what was being said, eg smiles and nods. He could have thought about his physical positioning in the group: could he be easily seen? Was he always the last into a room? John could have used the job specification to think up some questions prior to his arrival or ask follow-up questions linked to what had been said. He could always ask more general questions signalling his interest in the school, for example asking about after-school or residential trips. John should have engaged the children and adults with questions like these to signal an interest in them:

> » *Which class do you teach?*
>
> » *Whose class are you in?*
>
> » *Have you worked at this school for long?*
>
> » *What do you like about being at school?*
>
> » *Do you have to travel far to get to school?*

On school visits it is important that you demonstrate that you will be a good team member, and you can achieve this by giving examples through talking to the adults and children and by asking intelligent questions. You need to stand out from the crowd and make a positive memorable impression.

Making your experience show

Though you will be given help and support throughout your course in completing application forms or personal statements, it is important that you use relevant examples from your course and placements to support what you are saying. The person specification will indicate the essential and desirable criteria for the position. It will indicate how these criteria will be assessed, for example by interview, letter of application and qualifications. You must demonstrate in what you write that you can meet these criteria and that you are the right person for the job. In order to help you think about what you wish to say, it is worth going through your professional development portfolio or plan linked to your placements and academic record and reviewing how you have over the period of your course met and excelled against the eight Teachers' Standards (DfE, 2011c). You will then be in a good position to start giving concrete examples of how you may be the best person for the job. This is important since it will allow the head teacher or governors an opportunity to start to imagine how you might fit into their school to become a valuable staff member.

CASE STUDY

Fatima's personal statement

Consider the following excerpt from Fatima's personal statement.

The decision to make teaching my career choice was gradually decided over a few years. My experience has included many year groups but in particular a mixed aged Year 3 class. During this time I have learnt to use support staff to the benefit of all the children.

My professional development is very important to me and I am aware that this needs to continue throughout the whole of my teaching career. I look forward to the opportunities that your school will be able to provide for me in the future should I be appointed.

I believe that children should be given the opportunity to engage, achieve and flourish in their education. I believe every child is a unique individual full of potential. My role as their teacher is to support them in order to fulfil their true potential. My classroom management is based on a strong ethos of positive praise, consistent execution of clear rules, rewards and consequences. I ensure effective differentiation in my lessons, and use a variety of teaching strategies to appeal to a wide variety of learning styles.

I have a range of creative qualities that I draw upon in order to plan and teach good quality lessons. My strengths are in physical education, music, ICT and craft.

I enjoy and play various sports. I row, compete in marathons, play netball, football and am a keen surfer in the summer. I have volunteered for many youth camps and I am a guide leader.

Critical questions

» Are there any aspects of Fatima's form that could have been worded better?

» What do you think are the strengths of Fatima's application?

» What aspects of this application could have been developed?

» How does what she has written relate to the Teachers' Standards?

» Considering your own personal qualities, skills and experiences, what do you think you would be able to say about yourself? It is always a good idea to find time to start drafting your own ideas that may be incorporated into a personal statement. It is better to give yourself time to complete this task well rather than being in a hurry to create this vital statement quickly.

Comment on Fatima's personal statement

The first thing Fatima says is that she decided to make teaching her career over a few years. This sounds indecisive and suggests that teaching might not be her real vocation. Such an introduction to an application will fail to impress any vacancy panel. Fatima should state the aspects of being a teacher that she really values, showing her commitment and love for the job. Similarly, although it is good to state hobbies of a sporting nature, Fatima's extensive sporting statement might imply that outside school hours she will be very busy and therefore will have little or no time to commit to school events, clubs or the teaching profession as a whole. Such a statement fails to help an employer see how she might fulfil her *wider professional responsibilities* (DfE, 2011c, Teachers' Standard 8). Fatima should have perhaps just picked one of these hobbies and balanced it with something less time-consuming such as reading, going for walks or jogging. This has the added benefit of allowing Fatima to outline the benefits her hobbies may have for the school, such as establishing an orienteering club or reading club.

The strength of Fatima's application lies in her statement about children, which includes her core beliefs and values about educating children. It shows a real feel for children, their learning and her expectations for them. Fatima sounds as if she takes an inclusive approach and would be able to control any class she might be given. This clearly links to the Teachers' Standards (DfE, 2011c), in particular Standards 1, 2, 4, 5 and 7.

Fatima failed to develop a description of her experience or do more than mention the age range and abilities with which she has worked. She also failed to explain what she has learnt by teaching these age ranges. This makes it hard for prospective employers to see how she might fit into the vacancy. If it is for a particular age group she needs to not only focus on them but also on how versatile she could be if placed in other classes in the school. By mentioning a range of experience Fatima will show a better depth of understanding of the development of pupils. Fatima also neglected to capitalise on her curriculum strengths by not stating how they might be used within school, eg in the form of an after-school club. Fatima has not succeeded in showing how she might be suitable for the post and fit into school life. Fatima's wealth of knowledge and experience could have also helped her develop her application in relation to Teachers' Standards 3 and 8 (DfE, 2011c).

It is important in your personal statement that you do justice to yourself so you need to structure your personal statement well. By outlining and linking your personal qualities and strengths, your experience and what you have learnt, both at university and while on placement, to what is required in the person specification, you will be in a good position to start writing your personal statement. There is no one template that you can use, but you should cover the areas outlined in the next section.

Your personal statement

When writing your personal statement you should make references to the Teachers' Standards (DfE, 2011c). They may also be used as a vital checklist in order to make certain that you have covered all aspects of professional responsibilities and aptitudes. Though you must avoid repetition of information from your application form it is important that you state the following:

- your personal qualities, including your personal strengths;

- the type of school placements you were in and their duration;

- the age range taught;

- how you have developed your experiences through undertaking these placements and what you may have learnt, eg being able to cater for the needs of a child with a statement of special educational needs;

- your curricular knowledge, including professional development, alongside how you are able to plan, adapt and assess to provide for inclusive practice;

- your values and attitudes to education and the children in your care and how they underpin your practice;

- how you can manage behaviour effectively and your approach to behaviour management;

- how you have demonstrated a commitment to the profession and, if appointed, how you would demonstrate commitment to the school;

- your wider professional abilities, eg how you would work and communicate with parents and colleagues.

You will be asked to include the names of two referees and their current posts at the end of your application form. Your first referee will be from your current Initial Teacher Training (ITT) provider and you should contact them to discuss who this is. It is likely to be the head of your department, although academic tutors will have been involved in creating this reference. Your second referee should be the head teacher, mentor or senior manager from a placement school you have worked at. You will need to seek their permission before you leave the placement that they are willing to act in this capacity. Normally most professionals are willing to offer to write references; however, if they are not prepared to say yes you must consider why! Whoever the referee is, you must always ask their permission and always contact them if you have applied for a post. This means they will be expecting to be contacted by the school and will have time to consider what they wish to say.

Please remember that employers nowadays are very aware of the likelihood that applicants will have a Facebook account alongside the normal email address. Now that you wish to enter a vocation that requires a high degree of professionalism both while on the school premises and outside of school hours, you need to think carefully about what you may have posted on social media sites. Be mindful that everything put on the web may ultimately become part of the wider public domain, otherwise your reputation may be damaged even before your references have been taken up!

You could, however, make certain that any social media that you might choose to use is to your benefit. For example, LinkedIn nowadays has become an important job promotional tool whereby you can tell all those likely employers out there about your latest accomplishments and employment status; Twitter has a large education community, which includes influential professional educators and bloggers. Both may also be used by more web-savvy job recruiters as a means to locating ideal candidates. So why not make yourself known! However, as a note of caution, it is worth separating personal accounts from private ones and being aware of the public nature of such forums.

Interviews

If your application is successful you will be contacted for interview by letter and/or email. On receipt of this you should contact the school to say you are willing and able to attend. The letter from the school will outline the process and set out what is required of you. You will most probably have to be observed teaching prior to the interview or on the day with either a lesson of your choice or one set by the school. Do not be afraid to ring up the school if you are in any doubt about the process or if you need further information. Make sure you are clear about whether you are teaching a whole class or a small group, and how many children this will involve. Ask a tutor or another teacher to go through your lesson and offer suggestions regarding any improvements you might make. You will also be asked to bring your academic certificates with you to verify your qualifications, some photo identification and your CRB form.

Critical questions

» *What lessons would you ideally like to teach if someone was observing?*

» *Is there a lesson you have taught in the past that was very successful and might be adapted for the purpose of an observation?*

» *Where can you seek help if you are asked to teach a topic that might be unfamiliar to you?*

» *What sort of questions might you like to ask a school to clarify a teaching task you have been set?*

Arrive on time or, even better, slightly earlier than is set. On your arrival at school you will be told where you must wait and at this point you may be asked for your documentation and a contact number to be used after the interview. From arrival at the school to departure, remember you are at interview. Small talk with the school secretary can potentially have an impact on the decision of the appointment panel!

Your tutors will no doubt offer you practice at answering questions at interview. However, faced with the real thing it can be quite daunting. Interview panels will vary across settings but they usually include governors, along with the head teacher and perhaps other senior managers; there may be up to five or six people in front of you. Usually the first question you will be asked is to settle you down into the process, for example 'Have you had a good journey?' or 'What do you think of our school?'

Extended thinking

Consider the following questions set by a panel to a prospective candidate:

» *How would you set high expectations for learning in your class?*

» *How might you assess children's progress in your class?*

» *What do you feel your curriculum strengths are and what could you offer the school with regard to them?*

» *If you had a disruptive child in your class how would you deal with them?*

» *If you had a difficult parent at parents' evening how do you think you would manage the situation?*

» *What do you think you can offer to our school?*

Critical questions

» *What should the candidate do before they start answering the questions?*

» *What should the candidate include in their responses?*

» *Try preparing your own answers to each of these questions and practise saying them out loud.*

Before launching into any answer you should carefully consider the points you wish to include in any answer. By taking your time, or even seeking clarification to a question, you are more likely to provide a fuller answer. When answering any of the questions it is fundamentally important to answer what has been asked. It is also important to talk about your values, thoughts and opinions and use concrete examples from your own teaching experiences to illustrate how you would deal with the issues raised. The panel will be looking for someone who shows conviction, who will fit in with their team, who shows strength of character, who is a good communicator and somebody who is always willing to listen and learn.

Any panel will not be looking for the finished teacher and they will recognise where you are in your career, but they are looking for someone who will bring something new to a school, who will grow into the role and a person who enhances the team of teachers already on the staff. They will expect you to know about current issues and trends in education, so keep a look out for what is currently happening and be prepared to offer your views– but make sure you understand the context of your audience before replying!

Critical questions

»   *What are your views on the creation of academies and free schools?*

»   *Can you think of any major government initiatives in the last 12 months? What are your views about them?*

»   *What do you think about primary children being required to learn a foreign language?*

»   *Do you feel teachers should be required to work beyond the age of 60? If not, why not?*

Though not all schools will request a portfolio relating to your professional practice, it is a good idea to create one to bring to interview. Though the panel will probably not spend long looking through it, bringing a portfolio to interview indicates that you are eager to show your potential, that you are professional and that the job means a lot to you. It will also make you stand out from the crowd. Your portfolio should be well presented and could include photos of your classroom, examples of work produced by children for you, displays you are proud of, achievement/professional course certification, examples of lesson plans, tutor/class teacher observations and perhaps any letters of gratitude to you from parents (although do remember to ask if items included in the portfolio can be shared in such a way).

Once the interview is over it is quite common for you to be contacted by telephone later in the day in order that you may be given the result. If you are successful, this will be followed up in writing and may be conditional on items such as a successful medical assessment. If you are not successful, arrange to talk to someone at a later date in order to gain developmental feedback to help you in further applications. Try not to take it personally, and remember there is a post out there with your name on it!

Induction of Newly Qualified Teachers

Once leaving training you will be encouraged to start induction as soon as possible after achieving QTS status. This means you are in the best position to retain and utilise all that you have learnt so that you can put it into practice as a fully employed and qualified professional. Though induction is statutory for all newly qualified teachers in maintained and non-maintained special schools in England, including maintained nursery schools and PRUs, it is not a legal requirement in order for you to teach in an independent, academy or free school setting (DfE, 2014d). You can, however, legally complete your induction in these settings.

Statutory induction forms a link between your training at your ITT provider and the profession you are joining. It will provide you with professional support, usually through a mentor in the school, a personalised programme of development, and a means of assessing and monitoring your achievement against the Teachers' Standards (DfE, 2011c). It will often last for the equivalent of one full year (three terms), though this can be done by completing a term at a time if you are initially unable to secure a full-time post. It is the head teacher in conjunction with the appropriate body (depending on the type of school) who will be responsible for setting the length of your induction and recommending that you have passed or failed your induction period. This will be based upon an assessment of your performance against the Teachers' Standards and an expectation that you have consolidated your professional practice from that of initial teacher training and that you have met the Teachers' Standards consistently over the induction period.

The process of induction follows a very clearly laid out procedure (DfE, 2014d; also see Figure 11.1).

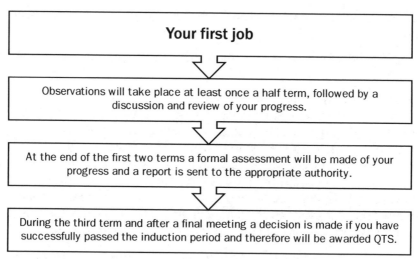

Figure 11.1 *Flow diagram outlining the process of induction.*

During your induction period your head teacher will ensure that you have a reduced timetable (no more than 90 per cent teaching) in order to complete activities relating to the induction programme. Your timetable will also be reduced, as with other teachers, in respect of planning, preparation and assessment (PPA) time. You should be observed teaching at least once every half term by your induction tutor and sometimes by others. These sessions will be followed by a discussion in which your professional progress will be reviewed. When you near the end of each term you will have a formal assessment meeting with your induction tutor and/or the head teacher. These meetings will be informed by the evidence derived from preceding assessment periods and also your work as an NQT. You should be kept up to date with any judgements made and this will mean that ultimately there will be no surprises. You should add any comments once assessment forms have been completed and then these forms must be signed by you, the mentor and head teacher; you should be given the original copy to keep. It is important that throughout the induction process and whenever assessments are created this process is kept confidential, and you should be made aware of who has been allowed access to these assessments throughout your induction.

During the first two terms of assessment your head teacher will have to report on your progress to the appropriate authority (normally the local authority); however, it is after the third meeting that a final decision is made and reported on whether you have successfully completed induction. This is then conveyed to you by the head teacher, who will contact the appropriate authority to formally confirm the decision.

Though it is important that you realise that relatively few teachers fail to meet the required standard as a newly qualified teacher, you will only get one chance to complete statutory induction. You will not be able to repeat this period (although you may appeal against a negative decision). Your name will also be placed on a list held by the Teaching Agency of persons who have failed satisfactorily to complete an induction period.

Planning for induction

In the past NQTs would use the career entry and development profile (CEDP) to reflect not only on the end of their initial teacher training, but also their early career development. Your school may choose to use this or something similar for the forthcoming induction process. You should have an induction tutor once you are successfully appointed by a school and they will provide you with an appropriate induction programme.

The CEDP is based around key transition points (TDA, 2011).

* **Transition point 1** towards the end of initial training, supported by your ITT tutors.

* **Transition point 2** at the beginning of induction, supported by your induction tutor.

* **Transition point 3** towards the end of induction, supported by your induction tutor.

For each transition point you will be given sets of questions designed to help you reflect on your progress and think about your future developmental and learning needs.

It is at transition point 1 that your professional development profile (PDP) constructed throughout your course will be used to create your CEDP. It is important for you to acknowledge that by the end of your ITT you will have come a long way from those tentative steps as a trainee teacher. It is by formulating your goals for the CEDP that you will be afforded a valuable opportunity to reflect upon what you have learnt on your course and throughout your placement experiences. It will offer you a basis for assessing your strengths and areas for future development and these will then be translated into goals for transition point 1. This will be done with you in conjunction with your ITT tutor in order to prepare you for the start of the formal process of induction at your school.

Consider the following questions presented to Laura when meeting with her tutor to set goals for her CEDP.

Critical questions

» *During your time at college, when writing assignments or doing subject audits, have you had any particular difficulties?*

» *Tell me about the successes and areas for development you have identified during your post-practice tutorials.*

»   *Is there anything significant in your observation reports written by your tutor, mentor, class teacher or head teacher during your placements which you are proud of or disappointed by?*

»   *What have been the areas in the Teachers' Standards you have found easiest to achieve or have needed extra support in order to achieve?*

»   *Why do you think the tutor is asking Laura these questions?*

The tutor is asking Laura all these questions so that she can reflect upon her own developed sense of professionalism during her time at college and on the course. The tutor is encouraging her to take ownership of her reflections, ready to begin the process of constructing the goals needed for her CEDP. Laura is being guided to think about all aspects of her training in order that the tutor may tease out the elements of her practice that may make suitable goals for her future professional development. By her own self-realisation of what she is professionally good at and in need of help with in order to develop in the future, the tutor is harnessing what hitherto might be seen as a reflective practice to inform her CEDP.

Extended thinking

If you were in Laura's position how would you assess:

»   *your professional strengths so far?*

»   *your own future professional development and aspects of teaching you wish to further establish?*

»   *aspects of teaching you have limited professional expertise in?*

Once the job of setting goals has been achieved you will be in a position to establish your CEDP. This can be created either electronically or in paper format. Remember it is there to meet your needs.

Transition point 2 will build on the goals you have set during transition point 1. Alongside your induction tutor, you will set objectives and create an induction action plan to provide a precise focus for future development. It will outline what further support is needed in order for you to meet these objectives while also detailing who will be responsible for what and when these items will take place. You will review and revise your action plan at professional review meetings and these will take place approximately every six to eight weeks throughout the induction process.

It is at transition point 3 that you will review your professional development over the complete induction period and acknowledge what has been achieved. It will provide you with a clear focus for your subsequent year of teaching and allow you and the school to plan for the prospect of being involved in the school's performance management process. This will be used in subsequent years to assess your professional progress and, if appropriate, to reward this success with financial increments if you are on the main scale, or with upper threshold payments (UPS) if you are beyond this point.

Chapter reflections

Remember to draw on the knowledge, skills and attitudes you have developed throughout your training to inform any applications you might make. When visiting a school, or constructing a letter of application or personal statement, consider how to make yours stand out from the crowd and demonstrate that you are the most suitable candidate. If you prepare thoroughly for your interview you will stand a greater chance of being successful. Be realistic about your strengths and any areas where you have developmental needs. This will not be viewed as a weakness; on the contrary, it will demonstrate your ability to be self-reflective, evaluative and critical, attributes that all good teachers should exude.

Critical points

» *Ensure you have thought about the age range, school and geographical area you wish to apply for before you start looking for vacancies.*

» *Your personal statement must be carefully thought through and is key to a successful job application.*

» *Ensure that social media is useful to your process of looking for a job.*

» *Ensure you are thoroughly prepared for any visit and/or interview.*

» *An analysis of your experience and key strengths and weaknesses will help you during the process of induction.*

Taking it further

Arthur J and Cremin, T (eds) (2010) *Learning to Teach in the Primary School*. London: Routledge.

TDA (2011) *Career Entry and Development Profile 2011/12.* https://www.gov.uk/government/uploads/system/uploads/attachment_data/file/181023/companion_guide-CEDP-TDA0876.PDF

Frequently asked questions

How far will I have to travel to get to my placement school?

This will depend on your provider; however, you should be aware that there is a national shortage of school placements and you therefore might have to travel up to an hour or 60 miles in order to get to your placement school.

Will I be in a school that is regarded as outstanding?

The majority of schools used for initial teacher training are those that are not deemed as in need of improvement or in special measures. Your provider will think carefully about your personal and professional needs and then assign you to a school that is appropriately challenging. For example, if you are an outstanding trainee you may be placed in a more challenging school in order to make a greater difference and to further develop your skills and competencies as a trainee teacher.

What should I wear when I am at my school placement?

You need to be dressed smartly, although wearing a suit is not necessary. You need to present a professional front, so jeans and a T-shirt are out! However, you will be undertaking, for example, art activities and therefore need to dress practically and appropriately for each event.

What if I am poorly? What should I do?

In the first instance you should always let your placement school know, as your absence will have an impact on your mentor and the pupils in your class. You should also inform your training provider so that they can keep a record of days absent. This is important, as you are expected to complete a certain number of days in placement in order to satisfy the Teaching Agency requirements.

Should I be part of a union?

This is very advisable as you will be entering a professional work context which can leave you vulnerable. You should ensure that you have joined a union prior to starting your very first placement. This will help protect you should an accusation be made against you.

What happens if the school closes, eg due to snow?

In the event of snow your training provider will provide clear guidance as to what you should do. Your health and well-being is of paramount importance and therefore you should not travel unless it is safe to do so. If the school is closed you might be requested to come into the college or university where you are training, or alternatively you may be directed to conduct some independent study. Whatever the circumstances, you should ensure that you keep your training provider informed of any closures or absences you might have in the event of a school closure.

I have no children with EAL in my class. How can I show I have a clear understanding of their needs?

For some initial teacher training providers their partnership schools are not necessarily bursting with EAL pupils. If you find yourself in this position you need to constantly ask yourself how you would cater for these individuals if they were present in your lessons. Reading widely and discussing these issues with your mentor will help develop your understanding of how to cater for EAL children even if they are not evident in your school placement.

How do I record the assessments that I have conducted through marking in pupil books so that I can demonstrate that pupils are making progress and inform my planning?

There are numerous ways of recording your assessments but you need to make these manageable and not onerous. Keeping records using a triangle or traffic light system will ensure that you are keeping a visible track of pupil attainment. In addition you may want to annotate planning after you have marked the pupils' books; in this way you are engaging with the planning, teaching and assessing cycle.

Glossary of useful terms and acronyms

AfL	assessment for learning. A form of formative assessment that is undertaken every day as part of the teaching and learning cycle.
AoL	assessment of learning. A form of summative assessment that is undertaken at the end of a learning cycle or academic year, eg statutory assessment tests (SATs).
APP	assessing pupils' progress.
CAF	Common Assessment Framework.
CEOP	Child Exploitation and Online Protection, dedicated to eradicating the sexual abuse of children.
Child protection	refers to the activity undertaken to protect specific children who are suffering, or are likely to suffer, significant harm.
CPD	continuing professional development.
CRB/DBS	Criminal Record Bureau/Disclosure and Barring Service.
DfE	Department for Education.
Differentiation	the way in which teaching activities and questions are organised to specifically suit the age, ability and aptitudes of individual children.
EAL	English as an additional language.
EHC	education, health and care.
EYFS	Early Years Foundation Stage, the age phase that incorporates Nursery and Reception.
Formative assessment	ongoing assessment conducted before and throughout every lesson.
G&T	gifted and talented. Gifted pupils are those who are exceedingly able in academic subjects. Those pupils with an outstanding ability in the arts or sports are regarded as talented.
HLTA	higher level teaching assistant.
IEP	individual education plan.

In loco parentis	means in the place of a parent. A teacher/school must show the same duty of care towards a pupil as would a reasonable parent.
Induction period	the first year in school as a newly qualified teacher, with lighter workloads, regular observations and increased professional development opportunities.
ITE	Initial Teacher Education.
ITT	Initial Teacher Training.
JSNA	Joint Strategic Needs Assessment.
KS1	Key Stage 1, encompassing Years 1 and 2 (5–7 year olds).
KS2	Key Stage 2, incorporating Years 3 to 6 (7–11 year olds).
LA	local authority.
Mentor	usually an experienced teaching professional who will be skilled in mentoring trainee teachers. Often they will have undergone mentor training at an ITE provider and be in a position to best support a trainee on a school experience placement.
NQT	newly qualified teacher.
Ofsted	Office for Standards in Education.
PDP	professional development profile, which contains the Teachers' Standards and supporting evidence to substantiate that they have been met.
Peripatetic teacher	someone who teaches in a number of schools, to give specialist instruction, eg in music.
PGCE	Post-Graduate Certificate in Education.
Plenary	time at the end of a lesson when the teacher finds out what children have learnt and reiterates the main points of the lesson.
PPA	planning, preparation and assessment.
Professional attributes	key qualities that a teacher should exhibit prior to, during and beyond training to teach, for example, honesty, enthusiasm, passion, etc.
PRU	pupil referral unit.
PTA	parent teacher association.
QTS	Qualified Teacher Status.
Reflection	an ability to be insightful about teaching and the teaching of others in order to inform personal and professional development as a teacher.
Safeguarding	protection of children from maltreatment so that children grow up in circumstances consistent with the provision of safe and effective care.

SATs	statutory assessment tests, statutory national tests in English and mathematics carried out at the end of Key Stage 2, in Year 6.
School Direct	an Initial Teacher Training (ITT) route that provides the opportunity for schools or partnerships of schools to apply for ITT places working in conjunction with an ITT provider. It offers two types of training, School Direct Training Programme (tuition fee) and School Direct Training Programme (salaried).
School experience file	a file comprising all the information needed for a placement in school, eg placement forms, a teaching timetable and lesson planning, observations and evaluations.
SEN	special educational needs. Children who have learning difficulties or disabilities that make it more problematic for them to acquire new knowledge and learning or to access education than children of the same age.
SENCO	Special Educational Needs Co-ordinator, who oversees pupils who have specific needs, to include those that are gifted and talented.
Simple View of Reading	focuses on two central areas: word recognition (phonics and high frequency words) and language comprehension, and underpins the significance of locating reading within an enriched curriculum.
Special school	a school for children whose special educational needs cannot be met within a mainstream school.
SSP	systematic synthetic phonics, an approach that relies on readers and spellers understanding how the sounds in words (phonemes) correspond to the way they are written or represented on the page (graphemes).
Summative assessment	sums up learning and occurs at the end of a sequence of lessons, end of term, year or key stage.
Teach First	a teacher training route for only the best graduates who commit to teach in low socio-economic schools for at least two years.

References

Arthur J and Cremin, T (eds) (2010) *Learning to Teach in the Primary School*. London: Routledge.

Bar, M, Neta, M, and Linz, H (2006) Very First Impressions. *Emotion*. 6(2): 269–78. http://barlab.mgh. harvard.edu/papers/VFI_emotion.pdf.

Bastiani, J (2003) *Materials for Schools, Involving Parents, Raising Achievement*. London: DFES.

Blatchford, R (2012) *The 2012 Teachers' Standards in the Classroom*. London: Sage.

Brookfield, S D (2002) Using Lenses of Critically Reflective Teaching in the Community College Classroom. *New Directions for Community Colleges*, 118: 31–38.

Brown, L (2011) *An Audit of the Needs of 268 Children Attending Pupil Referral Units in 4 Local Authority Areas*. www.ncb.org.uk/media/580252/matching_needs_and_services.pdf.

Carle, E (2002) *The Very Hungry Caterpillar*. London: Longman.

Chaplain, R (2003) *Teaching Without Disruption in the Primary School: A Model of Managing Behaviour*. London: Routledge Falmer.

Child Exploitation and Online Protection (CEOP) (no date) Thinkuknow. www.thinkuknow.co.uk/. Accessed 5 March 2013.

Clutterbuck, D (2000) Ten Core Mentor Competencies. *Organisations and People*, 7 (2): 157–71.

Cooperrider, D L and Whitney, D (2005) *Appreciative Inquiry: A Positive Revolution in Change*. San Francisco, CA: Berrett-Koehler Publishers.

Cremin, H, Thomas, G and Vincett, K (2005) Working with Teaching Assistants: Three Models Evaluated. *Research Papers in Education*, 20 (4): 413–32.

Cumming, F and Nash, M (2015) An Australian Perspective of a Forest School: Shaping a Sense of Place to Support Learning. *Journal of Adventure Education and Outdoor Learning*, DOI: 10.1080/14729679.2015.1010071.

CUREE (2005) *Mentoring and Coaching CPD Capacity Building Project: National Framework for Mentoring and Coaching*. London: DfES.

Day, C, Edwards, A, Griffiths, A, Gu, Q, (2011) Beyond Survival: Teachers and Resilience. http://www. nottingham.ac.uk/education/documents/research/crsc/research-projects/teacher-resilience/ beyondsurvival-teachersandresilience.pdf.

Day, C and Gu, Q (2007) Variations in the Conditions for Teachers' Professional Learning and Development: Sustaining Commitment and Effectiveness over a Career. *Oxford Review of Education*, 33 (4): 423–43.

Day, C and Kington, A (2008) Identity, Well-being and Effectiveness: The Emotional Contexts of Teaching. *Pedagogy, Culture and Society*, 16 (1): 7–23.

Day, C, Stobart, G, Sammons, P, Kington, A, Gu, Q, Smees, R and Mujtaba, T (2006) *Variations in Teachers' Work, Lives and Effectiveness: Final Report for the VITAE Project*. London: DfES.

DCSF (2008a) *The Assessment for Learning Strategy*. Nottingham: DCSF Publications. http:// webarchive.nationalarchives.gov.uk/20130401151715/https://www.education.gov.uk/publications/ eOrderingDownload/DCSF-00341-2008.pdf. Accessed 20 May 2013.

DCSF (2008b) *Talk for Writing*. Nottingham: DCSF Publications.

DCSF (2008c) *Personalised Learning – A Practical Approach*. Nottingham. DSCF Publications.

DCSF (2009b) *Achievement for All: The Structured Conversation Handbook to Support Training*. London: Stationery Office. http://dera.ioe.ac.uk/2418/.

DfE (2011a) *Support and Aspiration: A New Approach to Special Educational Needs and Disability*. www. education.gov.uk/publications/eOrderingDownload/Green-Paper-SEN.pdf.

DfE (2011b) *Achievement for All National Evaluation: Final Report*. www.education.gov.uk/publications/ standard/publicationDetail/Page1/DFE-RR176.

DfE (2011c) *Teachers' Standards*, May 2012. www.education.gov.uk/publications/standard/SchoolsSO/ Page1/DFE-00066–2011. Accessed 19 March 2015.

DfE (2012a) *Ensuring Good Behaviour in Schools: A Summary for Head Teachers, Governing Bodies, Teachers, Parents and Pupils.* www.education.gov.uk/publications/standard/Pupilsupportwelfare andbehaviour/Page1/DFE-00027-2012.

DfE (2012b) *Government Proposes Reforms to SEN System.* www.education.gov.uk/childrenandyoungpeople/ send/b0075344/government-proposes-reforms-sen/government-proposes-biggest-reforms-to-special-educational-needs-in-30-years. Accessed 16 April 2013.

DfE (2012c) *ITT Criteria Supporting Advice, November 2012.* www.education.gov.uk/ITTcriteria.

DfE (2012d) Provision Mapping. www.education.gov.uk/schools/teachingandlearning/pedagogy/a00199972/ provision-mapping. Accessed 16 April 2013.

DfE (2012e) Statutory Framework for the Early Years Foundation Stage: Setting the Standards for Learning, Development and Care for Children from Birth to Five. https://www.education.gov.uk/publications/ standard/AllPublications/Page1/DFE-00023-2012. Accessed 20 May 2013.

DfE (2013a) Alternative Provision Statutory Guidance for Local Authorities. Available at https://www.gov. uk/government/uploads/system/uploads/attachment_data/file/268940/alternative_provision_ statutory_guidance_pdf_version.pdf

DfE (2013b) The National Curriculum in England: Key Stages 1 and 2 Framework Document. https://www. gov.uk/government/uploads/system/uploads/attachment_data/file/335133/PRIMARY_national_ curriculum_220714.pdf.

DfE (2014a) Keeping Children Safe in Education. Information for All School and College Staff. Available at https://www.gov.uk/government/uploads/system/uploads/attachment_data/file/354151/Keeping_ children_safe_in_education_Information_for_staff.pdf. Accessed 4 March 2015.

DfE (2014b) Special Educational Needs and Disability Code of Practice: 0 to 25 years. Available at https:// www.gov.uk/government/publications/send-code-of-practice-0-to-25. Accessed 4 March 2015.

DfE (2014c) *Statutory Framework for the Early Years and Foundation Stage.* London: The Stationery Office.

DFE (2014d) Induction for Newly Qualified Teachers (England). Statutory Guidance for Appropriate Bodies, Head Teachers, School Staff and Governing Bodies. https://www.gov.uk/ government/uploads/system/ uploads/attachment_data/file/375304/Statutory_induction_for_newly_qualified_teachers_guidance_ revised_October_2014.pdf.

DfE (2015a) *SEND Code of Practice: 0 to 25 Years.* https://www.gov.uk/government/publications/send-code-of-practice-0-to-25.

DfE (2015b) *Research and Development Network: What Makes Great Pedagogy and Professional Development Final Report.* https://www.gov.uk/government/publications/research-and-development-network-great-pedagogy-and-professional-development-report.

DfES (2003) *Excellence and Enjoyment: A Strategy for Primary Schools.* webarchive.nationalarchives.gov. uk/20040722013944/http://dfes.gov.uk/primarydocument/pdfs/DfES-Primary-Ed.pdf.

DfES (2004) *Excellence and Enjoyment: Learning and Teaching in the Primary Years.* http://worldowiki. wikispaces.com/file/view/progression-9632.pdf.

DfES (2005) *Guidance for Local Authorities and Schools: PRUs and Alternative Provision.* www.education. gov.uk/publications/.../LEA-0023-2005-2.doc.

DfES (2006a) *Learning outside the Classroom Manifesto.* London: HMSO.

DfES (2006b) *2020 Vision: Report of the Teaching and Learning 2020 Review Group.* London: The Stationery Office.

Dinham, S and Scott, C (1998) A Three Domain Model of Teacher and School Executive Career Satisfaction. *Journal of Educational Administration*, 36 (4): 362–78.

Dinham, S and Scott, C (2000) Moving into the Third, Outer Domain of Teacher Satisfaction. *Journal of Educational Administration*, 38 (4): 370–96.

Education Select Committee (2012) *Local Offer. Pre-legislative Scrutiny: Special Educational Needs – Education Committee Contents.* www.publications.parliament.uk/pa/cm201213/cmselect/ cmeduc/631/63109.htm. Accessed 16 April 2013.

Ghaye, T (2011) (2nd edn) *Teaching and Learning through Reflective Practice: A Practical Guide for Positive Action.* Abingdon: Routledge.

Ghaye, T and Ghaye, K (1998) *Teaching and Learning through Critical Reflective Practice.* London: David Fulton.

Gough, P B and Tunmer, W E (1986) Decoding, Reading and Reading Disability. *Remedial and Special Education*, 7: 6–10.

Gravells, J, and Wallace, S (2012) *Dial M for Mentor: Critical Reflections on Mentoring for Coaches, Educators and Trainers.* Northwich. Critical Publishing.

Griffiths, V (2007) Experiences of Training on an Employment-based Route into Teaching in England. *Journal of In-service Education*, 33 (1): 107–23.

House of Commons (2011) *Behaviour and Discipline in Schools*. London: The Stationery Office.

Howard, C (2012) *The Influence of New School Buildings upon the Motivation, Morale and Job Satisfaction of Their Teaching Staff*. Unpublished PhD thesis, Birmingham University.

Kolb, D A (1984) *Experiential Learning Experience as a Source of Learning and Development*. Englewood Cliffs, NJ: Prentice Hall.

Kyriacou, C and Sutcliffe, J (1978) Teacher Stress: Prevalence, Sources and Symptoms. *British Journal of Educational Psychology*. 70: 85–96.

Loughran, J, (2000) Effective Reflective Practice, A paper presented at Making a difference through Reflective practices: Values and Actions Conference. University College of Worcester, July 2000.

McBer H DfES (2000) *Research into Teacher Effectiveness. A Model of Teacher Effectiveness*. Norwich: HMSO.

Moon, J A (2006) (2nd edn) *Learning Journals: A Handbook for Reflective Practice and Professional Development*. Abingdon: Routledge.

Morris, J and Woolley, R (2008) *Family Diversities Reading Resource*. Lincoln: Bishop Grosseteste University College. www.bishopg.ac.uk/docs/Research/Family%20Diversity%20Reading%20Resource.pdf.

Ofsted (2006) *Healthy Schools, Health Children? The Contribution of Education to Pupils' health and Well-being*. London: HMSO.

Ofsted (2008) *Learning outside the Classroom: How Far Should You Go?* London: Ofsted.

Ofsted (2011a) *Mathematics: Made to Measure*. London: HMSO.

Ofsted (2011b) *Removing Barriers to Literacy*. London: HMSO.

Ofsted (2011c) *Schools and Parents*. London: Ofsted.

Ofsted (2011d) *Successful Science*. London: HMSO.

Ofsted (2012a) *The Framework for School Inspection*. Manchester: Ofsted.

Ofsted (2015) Initial Teacher Education (ITE) Inspection Handbook. https://www.gov.uk/government/uploads/system/uploads/attachment_data/file/407861/Initial_Teacher_Eduction_handbook_from_1_April_2015.pdf.

Paton, G (2012) Ofsted: Teachers Packing Lessons with 'Bite-sized' Exercises. *The Telegraph*, 23 November 2012. www.telegraph.co.uk/education/educationnews/9683926/Ofsted-teachers-packing-lessons-with-bite-sized-exercises.html. Accessed 16 April 2013.

Rose, J (2006) *Independent Review of the Teaching of Early Reading*. Nottingham: DfES.

Schon, D (1991) *The Reflective Practitioner: How Professionals Think in Action*. New York, NY: Basic Books.

Steer, A (2009) *Learning Behaviour: Lessons Learned. A Review of Behavioural Standards and Practices in Our Schools*. Nottingham: DCSF Publications.

Stonewall (2009) *The Teachers' Report*. www.stonewall.org.uk/at_school/education_for_all/quick_links/education_resources/4003.asp. Accessed 16 April 2013.

TDA (2007) *Developing Trainee's Subject Knowledge for Teaching: A Way of Looking at Subject Knowledge for Teaching*. London: TDA Publications.

TDA (2011) *Career Entry and Development Profile 2011/12*. www.education.gov.uk/publications/eOrderingDownload/cepd_2011–12_tda0876.pdf.

UCET and NASBTT (2012) *Implementing the Revised Teachers' Standards in Initial Teacher Education: Support Materials*. http://www.ucet.ac.uk/3912.

University of Bristol (2008) *The Bristol Guide: Professional Responsibilities and Statutory Frameworks for Teachers and Others in School*. Bristol: University of Bristol.

van Manen, M (1991) *The Tact of Teaching: The Meaning of Pedagogical Thoughtfulness*. Albany, NY: SUNY Press.

Whitmore. J (2002) (3rd edn) *Coaching for Performance: Growing People, Performance and Purpose*. London: Nicholas Brealey Publishing Ltd.

Wilkin, A, Derrington, C, White, R, Martin, K, Foster, B, Kinder, K and Rutt, S (2010) *Improving the Outcomes for Gypsy, Roma and Traveller Pupils: Final Report*. London: DfE.

Wyse, D, Jones, R, Bradford, H and Wolpert, M A (2013) (3rd edn) *Teaching English, Language and Literacy*. Abingdon: Routledge.

Index

Some terms are defined in the glossary which can be found on pages 162–164. These page entries are emboldened in the index.

My notes and reflections